Into the Whispering Wild

First published 2025

Copyright © Hannah Dawn Gold 2025

The right of Hannah Dawn Gold to be identified as the author of this work has been asserted in accordance with the Copyright, Designs & Patents Act 1988.

All rights reserved. No part of this book may be reproduced, stored in a retrieval system, or transmitted in any form or by any means, digital, electronic, electrostatic, magnetic tape, mechanical, photocopying, recording or otherwise, without the written permission of the copyright holder.

Published under licence by Brown Dog Books and The Self-Publishing Partnership Ltd, 10b Greenway Farm, Bath Rd, Wick, nr. Bath BS30 5RL, UK

www.selfpublishingpartnership.co.uk

ISBN printed book: 978-1-83952-891-0
ISBN e-book: 978-1-83952-892-7

Cover and internal design by Andrew Prescott

Printed and bound in the UK
This book is printed on FSC® certified paper

Into the Whispering Wild

Hannah Dawn Gold

For Mum

This book is dedicated to my mother, for teaching me to live a life of inspiration and integrity. I am grateful that you showed me how to walk barefoot.

May you be blessed wherever you are.
May we meet again and know each other when we meet.

Contents

Prologue 9

Part 1 - *Restlessness* 11

Chapter 1 - *Storms and Rainbows* 13
Chapter 2 - *The Turning Point* 16
Chapter 3 - *Monty* 21
Chapter 4 - *Whispering Wild* 24
Chapter 5 - *Microcosm* 29

Part 2 - *The Inner Nomad* 33
Chapter 6 - *The Patch of Green* 34
Chapter 7 - *Places* 37
Chapter 8 - *Wild Sense* 40
Chapter 9 - *When the Rain Comes* 45
Chapter 10 - *The Battersea Triangle* 49
Chapter 11 - *Margins* 54

Part 3 - *The Lost Lands* 59
Chapter 12 - *The Edge of Land* 60
Chapter 13 - *The High Place* 66
Chapter 14 - *Thunder and Snow* 70
Chapter 15 - *What is 'Wild'?* 75
Chapter 16 - *The Lost Lands* 78

Part 4 - *We Are Dreaming* 83
Chapter 17 - *Messenger* 84
Chapter 18 - *Harvest Mice and Hoverflies* 89
Chapter 19 - *The Forest of Galloway* 93
Chapter 20 - *Red Kites* 98
Chapter 21 - *Moving On* 105

Part 5 - *South* 111
Chapter 22 - *Threlkeld* 112
Chapter 23 - *Dragons* 117
Chapter 24 - *Fire in the Hearth* 120
Chapter 25 - *Once Round 'The Wonky'* 124
Chapter 26 - *Mum* 127

Part 6 - *Returning* 135
Chapter 27 - *Midsummer Promise* 136
Chapter 28 - *Concrete and Serendipity* 141
Chapter 29 - *Barefoot Child* 148
Chapter 30 - *Beach* 155
Chapter 31 - *The Nomad's Hearth* 159

Part 7 - *The Adventure* 165
Chapter 32 - *Beyond Reason* 166
Chapter 33 - *Winds of Change* 173
Chapter 34 - *Sea Glass and Driftwood* 179
Chapter 35 - *One* 183
Chapter 36 - Two 187
Chapter 37 - Now 191

Prologue

Some journeys are intended. We know how long they will be. Others can grab us like a tide that sweeps us to another land, through an ocean of mysteries where we meet both darkness and light.

This journey started from one of those tiny openings of the mind that you don't see coming. Out of that chink of space, as if through some portal from a timeless place, a book emerged, like an animal, creeping from its lair and blinking into the sun. A living thing, grown from the wild world. Leading me to discover a new kind of home. One which is about our relationship with ourselves and the world around us. A state of being. Of aliveness.

Change is a journey too, perhaps the best one of all. When we change our inner landscape, other possibilities arise, which we would never otherwise discover. New horizons unfold and as we rise to meet them, we ourselves become renewed.

Part 1
Restlessness

"Until one is committed, there is hesitancy, the chance to draw back, always ineffectiveness. Concerning all acts of initiative (and creation), there is one elementary truth, the ignorance of which kills countless ideas and splendid plans: that the moment one definitely commits oneself, then Providence moves too. All sorts of things occur to help one that would never otherwise have occurred. A whole stream of events issues from the decision, raising in one's favour all manner of unforeseen incidents and meetings and material assistance, which no man could have dreamt would have come his way."

The Scottish Himalayan Expedition (1951), William H Murray

Chapter 1
Storms and Rainbows

November was a month of contrasts. Processions of howling storms hurled themselves against the rain-drenched edges of the land. They sluiced away any last vestiges of the soft mists that normally cover the Lizard Peninsula, rocking the caravan that had somehow unexpectedly become my dwelling place with Monty, my dog. Between the storms, vast rainbows arced across the coves and fields, dazzling yet fleeting against the perilous grey.

The Lizard is so named not because of reptiles, but because the name derives from 'Lys Ardh' in the old Cornish language, meaning 'High Place' with a subtler layer of meaning similar to 'High Court.' The name is apt, for the place has an unusually imposing air, beyond anything which mere geographical remoteness can afford, and it lends it a powerfully charged atmosphere. The last southward run of land in England before it drops away to the surging green sea. Long ago it would indeed have been high physically as well as by any status of importance attributed to it. The sea now covers what was once low-lying terrain further to the south. The tall cliffs of the Cornish coast are the remaining edges of ground which, if anyone had once been walking on those vanished lands, they would have looked up at, just as we now raise our eyes to the hills and mountains of our current landscape.

Tucked into a subtle fold of the land next to the ancient, grey farmhouse, like a secret within a secret, this well-hidden holt gave us welcome shelter and much more. It gave me space to rest, to think and at times not to think. To rediscover myself. I needed to shelter not only from the weather but from the world. Or at least from what I felt to be a falseness that was creeping across the world and from the tide of things that no longer worked or even made sense to me. Here I was to lay my soul at the feet of the wild world and hope for freedom with all the fervour of a prisoner seeking release.

A storm of changes had blown through my life, every bit as ferocious as the gales roaring in the treetops outside and although I welcomed change and movement, rest had become more than a necessity. I needed the kind of peace which comes only in the moment when you recognise that you can't deal with the way the world is any longer and realise you don't really have to. When you allow yourself to stop trying to do what isn't either necessary or meaningful.

The large log-burner in the corner was filled with bright golden flames that crackled cheerfully as if in approval of my stubborn independence from the slew of things that no longer made sense to me. The wind shrieked vehemently as it raced up the short distance from the sea, while torrents of rain hammered dramatically on the roof. Monty stretched out on the sofa next to me in delight at the warmth from the fire and waved his paws in the air in contentment. I gently stroked his silky ears and he murmured in sleepy delight as he nestled his head against my thigh. The purity of his love amazed me, as it has every day since he came into my life.

To outward appearances I am just another non-descript middle-aged woman, who no one would look at twice in the street. I like it that way. I relish my anonymity, having spent years cultivating it. I could be anyone. Sometimes I have been. I have a past and I hope I have a future. Whatever else is true, every time my dog looks at me, I know I have love. Possibly the truest form of love that exists on planet Earth, for no one loves with more wholehearted integrity than a dog.

I had never thought I would be homeless at the age of fifty. I've done the whole career success, big house and mortgage thing. I didn't know that when I set out to go along a different path, on which I could be more myself, that the shift of that pebble on the road of life would set off such a landslide of questions. On the other hand, neither did

I think I would have a friend as wonderful as Monty, from whom I could learn so much. I didn't know that a dog could remind a human who they are inside. But dogs see true. They see through all our masks and veils. They recognise our authentic selves. There are moments when a dog looks at us and the simplicity of their love is startling. It makes us remember ourselves as deeper, wilder, more alive beings.

It was a process that had begun some two years earlier…

Chapter 2

The Turning Point

Winter had come to the Fens, in the east of England, with the kind of slow, creeping stillness that somehow leaves us questioning all the things we hadn't intended to. The late December shadows stretched in all directions and as daylight grew dim, I reached inside myself, searching for alternative frames of reference. The questions didn't bother me but the thought that nothing might change and I might find myself repeating them year after year, winter after winter, that did.

An idea was flickering. Like the first leap of flames from kindling, the way they do at that moment when they can either ignite or wink out into darkness. It managed to slip past all the imprisoning expectations of my busy day, evading all the obstacles of thought and habit, where so many other ideas had fallen. Nudge, nudge… compelling my attention long enough to ensure I recognised it. The faint glimmer of my inner self, bidding me to come and find it from the scattered remnants of ideas and dreams I had abandoned along the way.

I didn't know that then. All I knew was that the outdoors was grabbing me by all my senses, trying to shake me loose from a trap of familiarity I had grown accustomed to accepting.

For months, it had been there, a vague uneasiness. It stirred every time I saw the pencils I never seemed to have time to use, or my easel standing forlornly in the corner where I never created anything. A hazy half-sleep seemed to have blanketed my senses in a mask of stuff that I had been telling myself was important. Daily, I walked past the pencils and turned away from the easel. There was always something else to be done, or I was tired and needed my bed before work the next day. But reality was about to break through the illusions and shatter them like eggshells upon the ground.

Behind the trance, the wild world had whispered, it had prodded, it had nudged and still I had walked away, because it was easier to live as the person who I had become rather than face the one I had left behind. Like an actor portraying a character, which, while it was not false, was not complete either. Until finally, the wild insisted.

A bitterly cold Friday afternoon in December was heading swiftly towards nightfall. Unable even to attempt to concentrate on work any longer, I switched off the laptop and put it away. Chains were starting to break, slowly. A will-o-the-wisp idea had been taunting me. I finally understood that it was far more important than anything I was pretending to be interested in doing and should not be ignored. It was trying to answer questions for me. Questions occupying the space behind the clutter clogging up my mind.

The previous night I had been standing at the side of my house. Icy gravel underfoot and a faint dampness sparkling in the air. A young crescent moon glittered bright and huge in a frosty sky. Hanging, stunningly paired with Venus twinkling above it in a pool of darkness, it had transfixed my attention. An omen of light. The sight would once have had me reaching for the richest of colours, to convey the intensity on canvas, paper or board. Before life had got in the way of creativity.

A compelling vision of brilliance, shining in icy midnight blue. I could have absorbed myself in it for hours but on that frozen night I had a young pup at my side, just a few months old and still susceptible to the chill. I picked him up and cuddled him. Warm in my arms, this tiny new life inhaled the frosty air and wriggled happily. We headed back in quickly. But something about that sight of the moon had stirred me, like a deeper breath of fresh, cold air or the shifting memory of some long-ago place, urging me not to forget.

"Draw again!" it teased. "Get out some paints. Pick up a pen! Whatever you do, remember this! You must remember!" Faintly, I knew that I must not let it slip away in the usual daily distractions of online calls, appointments and other people's priorities. Did I dare? In a quieter part of myself I sensed that the clarity of that moonlit night was a message that somehow would help with the changes I was making, even though I did not yet know how. It offered confidence and promise, even in the darkness of winter.

It felt so vital. I clutched onto it like a lifeline, invigorated by the vibrant image glowing in the deeper parts of my brain. Long-forgotten instincts and ideas stirred like creatures awakening from hibernation. Eventually, I went to bed. The image rested quietly behind my surface thoughts all the next day. Until, while I sat like a trapped animal, at my desk of tasks that were speaking nothing to my heart and longing to escape from the nonsense of the unreal, it broke back into my conscious awareness, riding on a wave of restlessness, bidding, "Draw me!"

I grabbed the first pen that came to hand and hesitating not one instant longer I started to draw the moonlit scene. "Stuff work! Stuff the laptop!" I muttered like a deranged person. "Stuff it!" Like a prisoner sensing an escape route through a window, enticed by the waft of fresh air after years in a musty cell, I scribbled words and ideas. I drew until I was sure, not just of the image but of the message it held for me and I was sure I would remember it. *This is real! Come back to the real places*! With that rough black-and-white pen sketch on a scrap of paper, I started writing too, drawing with words, and this book began to form.

That hasty sketch formed an exclamation mark in my life. A flow of imagery followed and the idea that maybe others too might be seeking a reconnection to the wilder world that used to both surround and fill us. I started to wonder if maybe there might be someone else, perhaps at a desk or behind an opaque office window. Someone, somewhere who, turning their face momentarily to the sky, also sensed a life outside the trap.

Were there others dreaming, not just of a holiday or long weekend, but of the urging call of a windy morning with haphazardly tossed clouds, of the taste of rain or the bite of frost on the skin? For the other than office-tame part of themselves to be given freedom from the screens, apps and false pretences of corporate politics and dramas that we so easily get lost in?

There is a world beyond those things. It was blowing back into my life like a storm, resurfacing from the ancient fens and flooding my senses. The wild world we all came from, that still resides in us and shapes us because it is what our brains evolved to attune our responses to. There are moments when we realise that these illusory furnishings of modern life are not only failing to provide for the full spectrum of our needs but are not even real. They exist, certainly, but they are without real substance. If we stopped feeding them with our attention, they would instantly evaporate. Stand on a hillside under a moonlit sky with the sweep of stars tumbling down from the depths of night, feel the force of a river or the bite of cold snow and you are once again amid what is real. The ceaseless chatter about meetings, appointments and other people's opinions is just white noise masking the real.

A river or ocean current is real. You can drown in it. A mountain range is real because you either find the pass between the peaks or you do not. So are the sun and moon because they warm the Earth and turn the tides. You can navigate by them, or you can fail to. The difference can mean your survival. The ongoing dispute at work, the constant, dragging issue that you wish would change, or perhaps the stress over a potential promotion or exam? While they might seem intense, if we stopped playing our parts in them would they still be there? Many would not. They would dissolve without attention like mist in the sunlight if we did not invest them with our focus. They are the creations of our minds. This doesn't always make them bad, but neither does it make them real until we make them so.

We have the power to call things from the realm of thought to the world of physical reality. Yet we use that ability haphazardly and leave the results to chance. The mountains on the other hand, would still rise and rivers still rush, the wind would gust and rain drum on our rooves, whether or not we heeded them. These are real. Spirit is real. The curve of a bird's wing, the soft spread of morning light burning away fog above a river, the colour shift of the sky at twilight, or the sting of cold rain. These can slice through the illusions, going on around us, without us, as we slip away from reality ever deeper into our virtual and artificial worlds. Where does it end? When technological entities create our world for us within an artificial space? Do we, ourselves, stop being real? Or forget that we ever were?

Chapter 3
Monty

Every now and then, someone comes along with the power to remind us of what is real. My someone was the tiny, black Cocker Spaniel puppy named Monty, who I had held close to protect from the cold that night. As if by some strange magic, his arrival in my life had coincided with my need for change. As soon as I had taken him home, I felt my awareness start shifting. I stopped and listened. I entered his world, his time frames, his reality. He was a living demonstration of the importance of trusting your instincts. I decided to follow his example and see what it could teach me.

Every day I was noticing how I had allowed myself to become shut to my senses. Until Monty shared that moonlit moment on the driveway with me. Daily, hourly, it was Monty who prompted my attention to reality. When Monty looked into the wind and turned to face the distance, I did it too, asking myself what he was aware of. Soon I realised that much of the time it is not that humans aren't capable of sensing things about the world around them but that our minds interfere and block what our senses tell us.

Now I was remembering to look up into the sky again, to smell the air more and be less preoccupied. Less separated from the world. In the depths of winter when Monty needed to go outside, I would often gather him against me, as I had that night, providing him my warmth, so that he could experience the outdoors a little longer.

I felt every stirring of his little body as his senses flooded his young brain with a deluge of information about the world around him. His furry muzzle wrinkled at new smells, his whiskers twitching delicately, filtering scents. His soft ears, even when at rest, still shifted their position gently at each new, tiny sound. The rustle of a restless bird fluffing itself in the sheltering hedge and the sound of leaves, all new to him, were fresh to me through his awareness, compelling me, "Pay attention!"

Unexpectedly, I was becoming rewilded and reawakened by my dog. It felt like being able to breathe fully again when I had been suffocating under the weight of office dramas, holding my breath just because it felt normal to do so. The supposedly real world was becoming thinner and more artificial by the minute, like a veil pulled over the deeper world or a virtual reality that we somehow forgot was only virtual and got lost in. *Bollocks to that!* I thought, emphatically. The more I realised how that suffocating shroud had wrapped itself around me, the more I instinctively rejected it. It felt like a sort of dying. Not the natural kind but falsely, where we slowly become dead by losing awareness while still inhabiting our bodies. *Fuck that!* My inner self recoiled from it like a bad smell. *Never again! I'm staying real now. My dog knows how. I can follow him.*

Monty was teaching me to listen again to the wild places. Bringing me back to life. He had much more sense and awareness than most of the humans around me. Watching him as he explored and learned, I realised that he was experiencing only the real world, not the fake. He wasn't interested in what people were trying to sell or talking about on social media. He wasn't worried what my colleagues thought about our team meeting. He didn't do politics or petty arguments and the only tweets he cared about were those of the sparrows in the bushes as he learned about the various creatures that he shared the world with. Watching him learn, watching the thoughts take shape in the expressions that crossed his little furry face, I became once again able to distinguish the real from the false and my tolerance for the latter, which was never high to start with, diminished rapidly to less than zero.

My puppy became my guide. Somehow it seemed perfectly sensible that he should be. He might be only ten weeks old but he was leading me to renewed awareness and I knew that learning from him was a transformational process which needed to be guarded and developed. I followed his example, using my instinct to hold onto that thin thread of reality as though it was a lifeline. Each time I took another step it got stronger. Although I didn't recognise it at the time, we were setting out together on the long road home.

Chapter 4
Whispering Wild

It was clear to me Monty could sense the wild in a very undiluted way. "Are we really like that too?" I asked him, "underneath all the diversions of our lifestyles?" Monty raised his tiny black nose to the winter air, prompting me to do it as well. When he did so it was a small and delicate gesture, sampling the air rather than inhaling just for the sake of breathing. I tried doing it the same way and found that when I did, it seemed to hold more small details. It smelled of rain and I discovered that I knew without having to think about it that the rain was several hours away and would not come in any measure until after nightfall.

Who are we? I asked, as I lay listening to the rain rattling on the window that night. I was starting to wonder, if I tried doing some of the things Monty did, could I increase my perception enough to come back to how I might have been if the world of cities, trains and computers had not intervened? How would it be if humans had not disconnected themselves from the Wild? Was anyone else also trying to find their way back out of the fog?

Who are we? I cast the thought upon the soft air and darkness. The night exhaled. "Who will you decide to be?" it asked me in return. "Who are you?"

"Hoo! ... Hoo!" echoed the tawny owl outside my window. "Who-ooo," blew the winter wind across the fens. I fell asleep. And as the cold gusts called to the owls outside, I started to wake up.

We would have to go soon. Change was looming before me like a mountain range that I had no idea how to cross. I had sold the house in a fit of determination to move on, though I knew not where I was moving to. I couldn't spend the rest of my life looking at the world through a gate, like a captive watching the sky from behind bars. I could no longer stay, standing at the end of a drive, just thinking about living, like a swimmer standing thinking about jumping into water, but not swimming. A fish doesn't look at a stream and think about it. A bird doesn't contemplate the sky, it just flies.

It was too soon. My mind was screaming in the background. Fear was beating at me like the gloom of the winter shadows. I just wanted somewhere to live for me and Monty. Somewhere smaller, so I could leave my job and hide somewhere quiet and green. I had moved house before. I even enjoy the process, but this time it didn't feel normal. It was more momentous somehow. As though I was standing looking at a landscape which I could not comprehend, somewhere I had never seen before, which didn't make sense. It felt right to sell, but after that there was only a void, beyond which I could not see.

Too soon I would find myself seeking a new place to live for us both, before I felt ready to. Having to ask Monty to go with me on many journeys, too frequently without knowing how to navigate the road ahead. "Ready?" I would ask myself. And my inner self answered. "Are we ever really *ready*? Believe in yourself and you will grow!"

Somehow that felt reassuring. It was OK that I wasn't prepared for this if I didn't have to be. If we were prepared for life all of the time, would there be a point in living it? How would we grow if nothing could surprise us? From deep within, a more ancient self was whispering, "You need this! Long ago humans moved on all the time. We could recognise when it is necessary to leave a place. You can't stay anywhere forever. I am your inner nomad. I am the one who has the skill to go without hesitation. Movement is one with life."

While he was just a few weeks old and still too young to walk outside on the footpath, Monty and I watched through the gate and I would try to guess at what he perceived. What deluge of information was flooding his young mind? The flat Fenland fields must have looked vast to him. Tiny little pup under those enormous skies. He would gaze out and look at me with quizzical brown eyes. "How far is it out there?" He seemed to ask. "Well, quite far," I told him. "But there are many, many more fields to find and very soon we will go and play in them. They are full of exciting things!" I continued, while he listened contentedly to the sound of my voice. "Birdies, trees, funny little bugs and all sorts of animals. Nice splashy streams for you to jump in. There's a great big Out There, out there, Monty! Very soon now we can go exploring and go on lots of journeys and adventures." He wriggled with happy excitement, wrinkling his brow as if thinking deeply. I had no idea how true my words were going to prove to be.

A flurry of small brown sparrows darted into the opposite hedge, chattering excitedly. They hid among the hawthorn branches, their voices subsiding to a half-hushed mutter, like playful children struggling to supress a secret.

With every passing day, our bond grew and with it, I dropped deeper into the act of noticing. December turned to January. My colleagues talked about our department's plans for the coming months and automatically included me, but I had already decided that I wasn't going to be there. I verbalised answers but my brain wasn't connected to the conversation. My need to escape was no longer a vague instinct permeating the edges of my thoughts but was fully formed and occupying my waking mind with conscious hopes. But some of it I couldn't plan because I couldn't formulate actions based upon too much unknown. I just had to start somehow, discover and let change grow from there. All my natural thought processes were being stifled and I needed to uncover them.

The January daylight was already starting to lengthen, slowly, incrementally turning the year onwards. Still, the arms of winter reached long over the wet roads and fields. A pewter stain seeped across a sky that seemed unwilling to shake off a wet blanket of cloud. But daily the freshening breeze grew a little more edgy, whispering subversively that winter would soon rescind its grip.

It would grow in strength until March came when it could blast away the wintery residue but until then, we waited, half submerged among the shifting clouds, for a change in season that we knew was coming but somehow still felt out of reach. The interminable tunnel of coldness that wrapped around the long months at the end of the year was cracking, prophetic shards of daylight splintering through the clinging dampness. The tiny, steady increases in brightness mirrored my own progress.

Just because I knew I needed things to improve didn't mean I knew how to achieve the improvements I sought. It felt much like trying to see the way ahead in those glimmers of daylight when each was the briefest glimpse of a rapidly closing window. But the light would get stronger and until then I knew the way to walk in the dusk is to reach out with all senses, not just vision. I had known this long ago but stopped doing what I knew. Life was about to give me plenty of practice in renewing the skill. I just had a starting point and a sense of direction. Plus, a dog. As it turned out, that was to be all I needed to find my way and I soon learned that the dog was the most important of the three.

Monty would demonstrate, over and again, an uncanny ability to find our way in places we had never visited before. If we stopped for a walk at a wood where we had never been before, I could say to him "Where is the car?" and even if we were far from sight of it, he would turn to run down a small track which to me looked improbable. Yet reliably, I found that if I trusted him and followed, I would soon see how it led to another trail which was the clearest way back.

He was always right. Sometimes startlingly so. If I ignored him and insisted that he followed me, he would look at me in bewilderment and then obey reluctantly, only for me to discover that I was the one who was wrong. I quickly started taking more notice. He knew not only when rain was coming but how far off it was. He always knew when walk times were, to the minute, but sometimes he would unexpectedly ask to go early. If I made him wait, inevitably we got soaked.

After a few drenchings, I finally figured out if I had gone when he said we should, we would have arrived home just in time to keep dry. He not only knew the rain was coming but had to have enough sense of how long our walk took, how far we went from home and when the rain would arrive to be able to tell me when to go. My trust in his senses and his ability to use them deepened by the day. *This is why mankind built a relationship with dogs. It is based on trust. They sense the way ahead better than we do.*

Far back in Earth's history, the human species was nomadic. We survived by hunting game and gathering food. We moved to places which held what was important to us, according to the provisions of location and season. From our earliest ancestry around eight hundred thousand years ago, to as recently as eight or nine thousand years ago, we lived this way. Those millennia imprinted on the human psyche the command, "Keep moving! If you don't like where you are, move to a better place!" To stagnate in one location is to stop being able to provide for yourself and those you care about and is to die.

Somewhere along that long journey, humans and dogs started to forge a partnership. We can't really be sure how long ago. All we can say is that our current evidence of that relationship goes back around fifteen thousand years. If it was longer we don't know. Now, that relationship was encompassing my days and wrapping itself around my soul.

Moving away from nomadic living has left an instinctive dichotomy deep in the human brain. A nomad understands that to remain in one place too long is to dwindle and die, because nowhere can sustain you in the long term. You must follow the herds of game and the seasons. You must not get left behind. A settled dweller learns to be rooted to a location because it provides what they need. Long ago, people learned that if the triangle of life, shelter, water and food, plus the vital addition of a defensible position could be maintained in one place there was no need to go. To travel was to take risks, to face losing what you had found, when it was comparatively comfortable. Since then, the competing nomad and settler within us have whispered in our subconscious brains the contrasting commands 'Go!' and 'Stay!' We still find ourselves torn by the impetus of each, even when we no longer recall their origins.

Chapter 5
Microcosm

Not all turning points in life have to be dramatic in order to have huge effect. This was small and subtle, but momentous, nonetheless. A quiet microcosm of midwinter stillness. I had walked down my driveway and stepped into another world. I feared it might slip away in the usual daily torrent, but despite its ethereal nature it felt too important for me to allow that to happen. It was a singularity. Minute but momentous. Conventional expectations would have had me brush it aside and 'behave myself' but I didn't feel like behaving myself. I felt the need to be able to breathe again. I didn't think I should have to conform to the expectations of others, just to feel like I could breathe freely. Suddenly, holding onto this emergence point felt as vital as the air in my lungs. Monty was my lifeline to sanity.

Everything physical was falling away as I packed it into boxes. "Is this what dying feels like?" I asked the sky. The dawning realisation of what matters and what doesn't. The sense of having to leave everything which isn't real, when the spirit calls us home. If so then I am not losing but I'm lucky. I'm learning that knowledge while still alive. I wasn't leaving but remembering. Maybe our souls are nomadic. My spirit had grown as restless as the wind that was stirring the trees in the lane. I doubt if I could have explained why, I just knew that I could no longer be what I had been. I couldn't stay where I was. Under that bright new moon, in the quietness of midnight covering the fens I had felt the breath of freedom subtly stirring and I could not let go.

Oak Tree was watching over the lane beside my house. Huge and still half robed in leaves despite the lateness of winter, Oak breathed rumours of older times and ways. "What do you want to tell me, Oak?" I asked and listened from within. A slight outward breath stirred, like something awakening that was half asleep. "You've remembered how to speak with me, young human," it murmured faintly.

"I thought you had all forgotten. No one speaks to me anymore. Long have I stood here before your ancestors were born, when mine were plentiful. My kind were everywhere. I was here when this thing you call a road was just a track where humans walked. Now they rush past in smelly metal boxes, always looking somewhere else. They don't speak with me. They don't notice my kin unless they think we are in their way. They never stop to look or listen. They never ask how I am or what I know." A long, slow moment passed while I waited, listening.

"I think sometimes humans just go to sleep inside," I told Oak. "I don't know why. They forget what they know. What they were born knowing." I waited and searched for the right words. "I won't forget. Wherever I go, I won't forget you or your kind. I will remember how to listen." A faint essence of hope and scepticism drifted through the winter air. "Let's see," murmured Oak.

With every day, a new conversation came. Or were they just newer threads in the same one? Each strand brought little pieces of awakening with it and with each my restlessness swelled like a seed waiting to grow. My inner nomad was compelling me to get up and seek the horizon and once I knew this it became impossible to ignore. Something far deeper and older was calling me home.

Although I had been planning some changes, I did not anticipate the magnitude of the shifts that were about to unfold. This would prove to be personal change on the tectonic level. Who knew one small puppy could have such a huge effect?

I knew the depth of my need for change but hadn't known that beneath it was the resurgent memory of wild places that I had once loved and lived closer to, before my concentration became absorbed in other things. I had left them behind and all but forgotten that I had done so. Now the world had become bigger again. My focus on life became wider, like stepping outdoors and seeing the whole sky, not just the view through a window. I remembered things I had once wanted to do before I walked in the grey world. I started to wonder again about what was possible, like a child does, while the scope of life still seems unlimited.

I needed to paint again and write too. I needed to explore and grow. I couldn't do that in an unreal world because any growth I made there would be as false as the world I inhabited. No longer could I allow my relationship with the wild world and with myself to be something that was squeezed into the corners of a life that only suited other people's priorities. This was a necessity, not something to be 'fitted in' when convenient.

The life I had always wanted to live years ago could no longer be a patch of green grass at the side of a road to somewhere else; fertile but ignored. Shock reverberated through my days when I looked at how I had been living and realised that I felt like I had been fading away. I had slid into the artificial without noticing and as soon as I became aware of it then it suddenly felt like water closing over my head.

This tiny moment of renewal in the darkest point of winter had spoken softly of possible futures. Because I had listened to it, it grew. I started to notice wild friends who I used to know but had stopped having time to see. Now they emerged from the winter shadows. Birch, oak, buzzard, bat, moth and hare. With each glimpse came an opening into their story.

Every arced wing above and quiet glance from the hedgerow bid me listen. I asked questions of wild things at every encounter and to my surprise they answered. Something shifted within me. As I started to ask what they wanted to say, their voices became clearer with each asking. Perhaps they always had been, it was just my own deafness that had stopped me from hearing.

With a jolt, I recalled that it hadn't always been that way. I suppose it shouldn't have surprised me at all as I had talked to them all the time when I was younger. I had just forgotten that I had done so. We forget so much of our real selves under pressure to conform to routines, rotas and schedules that it drives our wildness away, to wither in some half-forgotten part of our selves like a branch of leaves, severed from the tree that fed them.

Drawing that breakthrough, moonlit image was the removal of a stone blocking an inner spring. Ideas and words started to follow from it, as though the years I had spent looking the other way now transformed themselves into a flood of creativity. I drew Monty, I photographed him, I made notes. I happily used the best notebooks, which I had always been keeping for some project or other, without worrying about how the words sounded or whether anything was complete. Books started to form from the layers of images arising from some happier self whom I had almost left behind.

The year was ending but change was beginning. Sparks of memory, imagination and something more were combining together. I knew there was more to come, a bigger story to tell, and I wondered if perhaps the wild places wanted to be given a voice. The roots of that question grew and spread as if to form a bridge between the wild and the human worlds, asking me whether they were ever meant to have separated.

I should not have been surprised. The fens are ancient and the human experience there of living close to wild places is very long. The marshes are mostly long since drained. They have been turned into fertile farmland, all criss-cross woven with the ribbons of waterways. But even though the landscape has changed, the pulse of the land is easier to feel here in the open spaces, where the urban intrusion is minimal. It is as if there is something in the nature of the place that keeps the concrete, glass and tarmac at bay.

Part 2
The Inner Nomad

"It's a dangerous business, Frodo, going out your door. You step onto the road, and if you don't keep your feet, there's no knowing where you might be swept off to."

Bilbo Baggins in *The Lord of the Rings,* JRR Tolkien

Chapter 6

The Patch of Green

A memory surfaced, clear and strong. Vividly, the walk to my junior school sprang to mind, as though in response to my strengthening need for freedom. The short distance only took five minutes on foot but the route was an adventure of temporary freedoms which I wished could have lasted for miles. The quiet road between the two places cut across the middle of a small grassy area, dividing it into two small greens with houses at each far side.

In many ways it was a small and unremarkable location, but in the summertime when the grass grew taller and dried off, rustling in the breeze, it could free my mind for a few moments from the constraints of school and the already steadily increasing encroachments of artificial life. Although it took only seconds longer, whenever possible I would walk around the longer, curved side rather than directly across the middle, just so that I could spend just a little longer within sight of a green place and breathing the aroma of growing things.

I remembered it now, wondering whether this change had simply been coming inevitably since then. Since I had felt dragged away by an alien set of social expectations from all that was wild and green.

Every moment there in that small green space was about holding onto wildness. I knew by heart every tussock of weeds between the paving slabs, where nature seemed to be fighting for its right to exist.

I saw each small plant defiantly trying to hold back the concrete and I felt the same. Like the wildness in me was being forced into ever smaller spaces, creeping out only where it could squeeze through, unnoticed. Shining brown ants spilled from between the cracks in the heat of summer. Strands of shepherd's purse and coltsfoot were a welcome joy. To find the occasional cat in a front garden, tail curling and yellow-eyed, was equal to greeting a mythical being. Grasshoppers, singing in the height of summer, were chirping, lime-green miracles.

This green area I passed daily was just a small grassy patch, in a nondescript street, not particularly rural, but to me it was the freedom of the almost-wild and I hated having to walk by. I longed to sit in the middle of it, wondering whether, if I could say the right spell, would the built-up world recede and the grass expand all around? Until it rolled in all directions as an ever-flowing savannah of green waves? With me surrounded by it, breathing the land and watching the sky through a thousand nights and days. I sensed the demand to let go of the wild pervading my world, taking parts of me away with it each time I obeyed. It was slowly dawning on me that wild nature was seen by many as inconvenient, dirty, or somehow disturbing and that our wildness, like the grass in the paving cracks, was fighting for the right to exist. People would prefer it to be sanitised, polished and shiny rather than simply what it was.

Like a clump of grass amid the concrete I had suffocated and survived for years since then. Until decades later, my puppy and I were setting out on our journey to find a new home and one of the things I knew I needed to find for us was a place that was more than just a patch of green. The wild places that remain in all of us were suddenly speaking loud and clear again. The big Out There was inviting us to step into it and grow, with the discovery of all types of new horizons. I knew without doubt that whatever happened I could not give up the green places again, especially not the inner ones.

I had thought we were looking for home, but that seemed elusive and I wasn't sure why. I resolved that if I couldn't find it then I would search for wild places instead. Perhaps the wild would bring me home. Perhaps 'Home' wasn't what I thought it was. Uncertainty jolted the framework of my thoughts apart as I realised I wasn't sure. Until I knew what it was, how could I be in a position to know where it was? How are you ever to know you've found something unless you can recognise it when you do?

Into the Whispering Wild

Chapter 7
Places

Sometimes we find places of a kind where it almost seems better to term them 'Places' with a capital 'P.' They don't bear names or titles, nor is it possible to describe their significance by way of physical characteristics that are readily explained. Not in cultures that have forgotten how to recognise them. They have other qualities. We encounter them randomly. These are spots we find ourselves drawn back to even when there is no easy or logical explanation for wanting to be there. We walk a longer way home, just because there is somewhere on the route where we feel better for having been. We take a slower path, it crosses a bridge over a river and the estuarine view opening towards the sea makes the heart sing, in any kind of weather. Grey is an enchantment in such locations as the mind opens to see deeper layers of the world beyond the immediate.

Children know this naturally. They sense the wild in an unhindered way, for it is latent in all of us. It was a latency I was starting to recall. The way we experience life before we start to question it. The evolutionary timescale is vast. As a species we have spent hundreds of thousands of years without changing a huge amount biologically during our development from the earliest nomadic hunter-gatherers. By contrast the time we have spent living as we do now does not even equate to the blink of an eye.

While it may seem that our lifestyles as we know them have existed almost forever, they are in fact extremely recent. So, the wild world speaks directly to older parts of our brains. Sea breeze, scent of rain on the wind, glow of sunlight behind clouds. These are the things which our older, wilder selves understand.

I had discovered one Place when out walking in the Fens. I turned off the lane that led past my house and took a track across open fields that was nothing more than a muddy, stony edgeway between an expanse of uncultivated field and a drainage ditch. Drawn by the open view on the far side of the span; I gravitated towards a small intersection, where the footstep-wide trail crossed over a tributary to the river Ouse, by means of a small footbridge. They formed a natural crossroads of barely visible footways and water, under the open sky.

Many might see nothing here and walk right on past. There is just the track and the slightly tatty bridge. There are no roads, shops or immediate buildings and the nearest made road is just a small lane to the local farm. To an observer looking for the trappings of modern life, there are few to be found. But it is exactly that absence of things, that no-thingness about it that frees the senses from their incessant distraction. In such places our brains can work properly again, the way nature intended.

At times, the area around the bridge is almost cocooned in an absence of man-made noise. Almost. Some distant vehicle noise makes an unwelcome punctuation to the peace, but at some times of day even that recedes momentarily. Dogs bark intermittently and cockerels crow at the nearby farm but there is less auditory clutter. Just like at night when senses suddenly expand to cope with the temporary absence of detailed visual information and we become more aware with our other senses.

In the summer, the early rising sunlight falls quickly on the land here and is late to leave it because the horizon is so exposed. On the approach to the bridge, the grassy track widens and rises slightly towards the wooden arch that lifts it across the river. A small, undecorated span of weathered wood, raising a question mark of direction. Do you cross and rejoin the lane to the next village, or take the wilder trails beside the river?

Here at this joining point of land and water routes, where reeds, sky and water stretch in all directions, our dichotomous relationship with the wild world is stark. Only if you turn off onto the riverside trails or find little-used tracks through the fields can you avoid returning to where the artificial world encroaches once again and if you do so, these paths always seem too short. The next road is only three fields away. These bubbles of reality are becoming like those tufts of grass between the concrete slabs on my childhood journey to school, surrounded by a creeping invasion of buildings, roads and fumes. The mask over the real world that we tell ourselves is normal.

We have been losing ourselves slowly. Our brains developed to assist us in living effectively in the wild. They have not changed to catch up with the recent technological demands upon them. But now there are constant new demands and under pressure we have to push something aside. The loss leaves some abilities underused while others are overstretched. An imbalance occurs, unsettling, and all the more so when there is little or no acknowledgement of where it stems from.

Our wild roots are treated as inconvenient. We have got used to things the way they are. We have been falling asleep. It can be difficult to imagine that not only did we live very differently but we did so only a short span of time ago and our brains are still attuned to an environment from which we have detached ourselves. Those brains are hardwired to protect and provide for us. They have developed around ways of understanding our environment and our place in it, via the senses that we reach out with for information. As well as the five commonly recognised senses, there are others. One of them detects Places. A bit like having a personal sonar system. Our wild-sense.

Chapter 8
Wild Sense

Within us is a quiet inner space, clear, like a deep pool in a forest. This is where our wild-sense lives. As real as hearing, vision and smell. As strong as touch and taste. It detects what is around us; it tells us of movement, proximity, Places, changes, objects in the road ahead or on the horizon. The clearer the pool the more it can detect. Footsteps cause tremors which ripple the surface. Events begin to unfold and even before we reach them, their images cause reflections and shadows on the pool within. When we are clear and attuned, we notice the ripples.

We have developed senses to understand the natural world. Our wild-sense is one of those and if we disconnect ourselves from it then we force ourselves to live with an absence of information. Information which over hundreds of thousands of years we have judged necessary to provide our protection. The pool clouds over. The wild-sense dwindles. To our deeper minds that absence of awareness implies vulnerability. Slowly I began to wean myself away from the distractions of the unreal and in doing so I became ever more unable to pay attention to them. I couldn't go back. It would have felt like willingly returning to prison after having escaped.

In the fens in winter, everything is half seen. The land excels at mystery. It looks flat at first glance but is a textured tapestry of subtle layers, like the sea. In winter they shift with the mist and low light until the senses have to adapt to cope with the ambiguity. This is a landscape to sense, not see with conventional focus.

More memories of past learnings came floating back, like shining pebbles uncovered by a river. In traditional Budo, the Warrior's Way or Path, there is a concept of 'Zanshin,' which approximately translates from the Japanese as 'remaining mind' or 'lingering mind'. It describes the state of awareness that exists beyond our conscious thought. It is the place we can act from without pausing to think. In Japanese culture this is something that human beings possess innately and therefore is not something we learn to do but remember because it was always there.

In Western culture a similar frame of reference is referred to as the subconscious, a psychological term used to describe a powerful awareness existing beyond the conscious state. Whatever we call it, one thing is clear. The brain is capable of perceiving and interpreting vast amounts of information, infinitely greater than the narrow band of focus that our conscious minds provide. The fens are a landscape which brings the remaining mind to the fore.

Our brains evolved over hundreds of thousands of years to sustain us in the wild world where we developed as a hunter-gatherer species. They function on these different levels for good reason. Living as hunter-gatherers it was essential for us to be able to see food, changes in the weather and potential dangers through a three-dimensional plane before they reached us. We make sense of our world in a multi-dimensional way. The connectivity between our eyes and brains developed accordingly, to enable us to function effectively in the real, physical world of forests, rivers and mountains, not in an artificial one of screens and apps. I didn't know why the world was getting so masked with all these layers of falseness. All I knew was that wherever I tried to use any process which involved engaging with another human being, I was continually being told "You can use our app for that!"

In our remaining mind resides our connection to the wild. Our inner selves are not in an app. Screens are two-dimensional and a lot of information we naturally seek is left out. So, while we are watching them, parts of our mental capacity are doing far less than they were intended to. Or sometimes are being made to function in a framework that they are not best adapted to make sense of. We have always had large amounts of our remaining minds 'remaining' just so that they could do exactly that, remain and filter the vast amounts of information we are surrounded by without us having to think consciously about everything all of the time.

Realisation was creeping, slowly as the winter dawn. I was beginning to notice that the technological lifestyle numbs awareness of the functions of the remaining mind. It chokes off the connection to it, as though creeping tendrils of electronic awareness had infiltrated thought itself, crossing the interface from being usable tools to invading consciousness with computer code. Is it any wonder so many mental health problems abound in our culture, as volumes of people grow subliminally uncomfortable with the technological intrusion that supresses the natural capacity for thought?

Too much tech doesn't empower us, it disempowers us and destabilises our full array of mental functions. Monty knew better. He did everything wholeheartedly. He played, hunted and slept entirely in the real. When he woke and looked at me it was with eyes filled with unconditional love. His perceptiveness, of real reality, not pretend reality, was a revelation.

In the past I had chosen to willingly accept the daily pressures of reports and spreadsheets, for reasons I was glad to uphold. But whatever my conscious mind had been taught to consider as important priorities, I knew that my remaining mind didn't care about most of them.

The remaining mind dwells in a state of guardianship, processing all available data for the purpose of keeping us alive. It has an entirely different set of priorities. "Can I navigate?" it asks, as it monitors our surroundings, "Can I find shelter and food? What is around me? Am I safe from threat? How can I leave if I need to?"

It takes in everything it can. It entwines with the wild-sense. It evolved to rely upon input from the wild and when key sources of information are absent or hard to access it dwells in a sort of no-man's land of lost detail. A place where the wind doesn't blow, and light follows no rhythm. But in the fens the wind blows almost permanently.

Even at the darkest point of winter the skies are so wide that despite the lingering mists the light hours never seem quite as short as they do elsewhere. It is easier to pick up the direction of the returning sun where the land is so open.

We innately seek the means to understand direction. With the loss of the horizon and natural light our brains have become deprived of navigational information. Even though we seldom need this now to find our way home. It is not essential for using a train or bus, but we still search instinctively for the information the horizon contains because our brains are demanding it, whether we pay attention or not.

In office buildings with windows obscured with tinted glass and blinds, the brain screams "Where is the daylight?" When functioning long term in a subliminal level of sensory deprivation, our inner compasses go slightly haywire, constantly calling for frames of reference: "Where is the sky? I can't see where I'm going. I can't smell anything. There is no information here from the air! What is around me?" Through all of this the wild world speaks and breathes of freedom. Not separate from us, not external, not an afterthought or an incidental but part of us.

Now I realised that in the offices of my city-based work, through the months that stretch into years, my brain had been reminding me that I had stepped into an unreal place, and it needed the horizon again. It needed those wild frames of reference, asking me for them until I came to acknowledge with some urgency that I couldn't do without them. I could no longer navigate through my life, just as my brain was unable to navigate in the urban landscape in ways that came naturally to it.

I could understand how I had come to that point. Life can be seen as a series of stages of letting go, but somewhere along the way I had started letting go of the wrong things for no better reason than because our way of living demanded it.

I had let go through all the years of forgetting, through the slow, weary attrition of the real self, until one day I found myself working in an office where I used to arrive earlier than most of my colleagues.

The first thing I would do was walk to the windows nearest the bank of desks where I sat and open the blinds to let in the daylight. I would get about half an hour if I was lucky, before predictably the next people would arrive and promptly shut them again, complaining it was too bright or there was too much glare on their screens.

More like too much reality, I thought, watching with curious frustration. I understood the inconvenience of screen glare but it was such an automatic rush to the windows to exclude the light as soon as entering, before even stopping to get a morning tea or coffee, that it seemed as though it was the very sight itself of the outdoors which was uncomfortable. As though they could not bear seeing what they were disconnected from. A strange gulf was widening between me and most of the people here. I felt lonely. I was here but I did not belong. I knew this was no longer my place and that knowledge felt like a fresh breeze had managed to sneak in past the carefully blocked-out windows and stir the air in this stale place.

Chapter 9
When the Rain Comes

There are Places the world over. I've found some of them. I'm still looking for others. The wild is stronger here, the pulse of life-force from the earth slightly more powerful, even when the human influence is great. Not always the obviously wild locations, they can turn up mostly anywhere we might encounter in daily life. Maybe in a patch of green. Some of them are untouched and others are trying to survive. Sometimes wildness is a consistent presence, at others it emerges in a momentary flash when the real world breaks through. I've always wondered why some people are drawn to linger and others hurry to get away or skirt round them. It is as if some older energy in the land transmits an inbuilt signal which either attracts or repels.

Yes, there are Places in the shaded woodlands and rugged coastlines, but they can be found in a random field. Or revealed by a blaze of sunlight bouncing off a river amid glazed office buildings and the sudden breaking of summer heat into heavy raindrops drenching the city footways, sluicing the baking tarmac roads with freshness. A wet slap in the face from the real world, trying to jolt passers-by from screen-obsession, yelling silently to them, "Look up! At the sky, at the river! These are real, like the rain that is making you wet!" I had watched them, putting their heads down, cursing the rain which made them return their phones to their pockets. Walking faster, to escape from the touch of the real more quickly and return to a place where their screens would be safe from getting raindrops on them, so they could plug back into the electronic intravenous supply line of illusion.

The rising evening wind spoke true. The seasons don't deceive.

Autumn's first breath tries to tell us to pay attention to reality. Deeper, like the flow of a river beneath the leaves on the surface. The abundance of summer drops away and underneath we see the bones of trees and stones exposed. Reminding us to come back to the roots of who we are inside.

We have been driving the wildness and magic from the world. Covering it with concrete and plastic convenience, hiding it behind appointments and calendars. Confusing our senses with make-up, perfumes, sprays to supposedly 'freshen' the air and the incessant jibber-jabber online of who thinks what about something we would never even have heard of if it wasn't for someone trying to convince us that it matters just to increase their sense of self-importance.

But every now and then reality breaks through and quite often it does it in a Place. Real reality, that is, not what often passes for it in our endless virtual creations. Sometimes it just knocks quietly on the door and at others it insists with more emphasis. Perhaps we should pay more heed to those quiet knocks, lest the wild become unwilling to be ignored and force the door.

When we lose the love of the wild, then the part of ourselves that only lives and breathes when it can entwine itself with wild places starts to die. We become less than whole beings when we let the wilderness fade from our hearts. We turn into plastic people, driven by marketing into a frenzy of panic when we are short of products that we don't even need. Every little bit of wilderness that slips away lessens our ability for self-awareness and growth.

We lessen our future potential every time we diminish our wild roots. Wondering at the sparkle of light on water we sense those roots in our deeper selves. It's not an intellectual response. Even those who think they don't care about the wild can't help reacting to it. Why does the power of a storm make us breathe more deeply if not because it is only when we are aligned with the power of the natural world that we ourselves are most alive?

We still seek wildness, despite all our efforts to sanitise and digitise our lives. Our hearts start to die in its absence. We search for it not because it is something external, to be desired, but because the connection to it is within. An integral, forgotten part of ourselves. Inside ourselves we know we are not made of plastic. From within us the wild whispers and prompts us to remember. Even those of us who do not think of ourselves as the slightest bit outdoorsy cannot escape the history of how our species has developed or the effects upon us.

It is natural that we have sought all the benefits of progress. But humans have a tendency towards the short-term perspective. We often let our actions go too far without thinking what effect we have on our world or even upon ourselves. If we don't immediately see something right now, we tend not to want to acknowledge that it is there. But when we let ourselves out from behind the incessant adverts and deluge of viewpoints splayed across the media for widespread consumption, we remember what we always knew; that wildness is part of the world like we are.

We are one with this world. We cannot truly tame the world because it was never meant to be tamed. If we do, we will destroy ourselves with it, from the inside. We grew this way as a species. We can't shield ourselves from something intrinsic to our nature. Not if we are to truly evolve and survive.

This is why we feel lost without the wild places. A loss even more acute when we forget what it is that we have disconnected ourselves from. It spreads into a vague, discomfiting uneasiness that seeps through at a more fundamental level than our mental preoccupations. Stirring at the corners of our dreams, flowing from a time when we knew that we were more than just calendar appointments, reports and transactions. A time that sometimes we bury and then forget that we ever knew.

The wild-sense is the voice of our older selves and the heritage of the nomad. It activates in response to Places, still speaking from some deep, ancient part of our brains or DNA as though responding to the intangible ping of a subconscious radar system. The human brain has many aspects that we have not even begun to properly understand and a great many of us now live in ways which do not require us to use our senses to the extent that was once essential.

Our sense of smell, vital for survival to a hunter-gatherer testing the suitability of new foods, has become so underused that many of us can't even recognise basic smells or identify whether something in the fridge has deteriorated or not. We throw perfectly edible food away because a label tells us to or eat something which has gone off because the label says it should be fine. So infantilised are we by the disuse of our senses that we no longer trust ourselves.

The indefinable trace of rain drifted through my childhood, infusing the shifting air with a faint, unique scent some time before it made its presence felt physically. I danced in it when thunderstorms broke the long heat of summer with the blessing of huge, cool drops that washed away dusty sweat. The aroma that rose from the grass first thing in the morning with the evaporating dampness of the night. The smell of beech woods under the cooling canopy of branches. Smell is a part of our sensory repertoire that we have learned to relinquish in favour of written directives, but just like our wild-sense it is still there beneath the surface of our habitual thoughts and still it is trying to teach us. It can renew our connection to the real world if we let it.

We lose ourselves in dusty places, where the windows are always closed. But when we step outside and the rain comes, it speaks of life. Rain knows the oceans, the rivers and sky. Rain is the primordial song of renewal. Rain is the voice of our ancestors' memories. The winter rains were dissolving away all my layers of people I had thought I needed to be, like washing paint off a statue to reveal the natural form underneath.

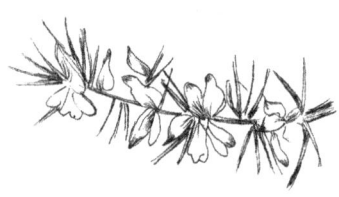

Chapter 10

The Battersea Triangle

Places don't have to be big or rural for wildness to come to the fore. Quite often they are nameless, just sort of *there,* in between other places which are mapped and named and recognised. It is almost as if they don't quite exist fully in our world any longer.

Or maybe they are in more than one world, and so they have a sense of transition about them, a hint of connection to other worlds and planes elsewhere. As though stepping off a kerb edge we could somehow fall through a doorway to somewhere else that we knew once but forgot. Somewhere in the act of stepping through that mist-thin boundary of consciousness between perception and the knowledge that there is more than we perceive, we rediscover our fuller selves.

A patch of rough ground that no one seems to pay attention to. Next to a road, or at the edge of a car park. A scrap of freshness that has escaped being built upon. Echoing the corners of our minds that we haven't filled with distractions. Even just somewhere that the breath of wind can catch the face and stir the patch of grass. A higher place away from street level where the air moves a little more freely, even if it is only on a city balcony. Somewhere that reveals the shape of the land. Somewhere our eyes can watch the sky-framed movements of cloud and bird. Each one a messenger telling us that the wild world is there if we just turn our senses to it. We look away to distract ourselves, but the grass still waves to us from the margins of the road and our wild-sense tugs at our hearts. The pool is still there beneath the piled-up illusions which have fogged it, waiting to be cleared.

Some years before, while I still worked in the concrete world,

I noticed a certain spot not far from Battersea, which the train approached on my regular commute. On the seemingly interminable trundle into Victoria station, there was a small triangle of ground, like an island, almost cut off from everywhere else by railway tracks and a long, dark wall.

There, where the city had almost covered everything under a tide of construction, grass had a hold, somehow defying the metropolitan stranglehold. A little bit of wild, forcing its way through and daring us to notice it. No one ever appeared to pay the slightest attention to it, despite the fact that the train crawled through at a snail's pace. I looked at my fellow commuters, wanting to ask them "Why don't you look up? Why do you not look at the sky?" The Place seemed to be hiding in plain sight.

I found myself wishing I could just vanish from the train and reappear there, unseen and unnoticed, like a beetle or a brown mouse. The trains and weary commuters would just pass by and I would sit on the ground looking up at the patch of sky, feeling the dusty land in this small spot that the layers of buildings had not covered. If I melted into it like some shapeshifter and I willed it enough, might the city somehow evaporate and that tiny triangle rematerialise in another place? Perhaps in an earlier time, before London arose in that landscape from the reed beds of the ancient estuarine marshes. Or perhaps just somewhere that the grass could spread freely again?

Here it stood, covert and almost completely unnoticed, defiantly wild, ignoring the city pouring its rush of trains and steel around it like molten metal. Barely holding on, surviving on invisibility. A little breath of green, almost suffocating in the grey tide. A tide that each day I would plunge myself into and swim for a while but never belong to. I too knew what it was to survive like the patch of earth. Wearing my city clothes, but green inside, I had lived the chameleon life in London for some time, just because it was where my abilities and ambitions had taken me. These small patches of half-seen wildness hover at the edges of our conscious vision. A corner, a forgotten space, perhaps a verge. You might know of one somewhere. Perhaps you've felt it nudging at the corners of your mind, trying to slip between your thoughts and draw your attention, whispering or even daring you to notice it.

In London, on the Embankment, a river of traffic pours a daily torrent of vehicles of all descriptions within a stone's throw of the Thames. I know some parts of the stretch of the river between Vauxhall Bridge and London Bridge particularly well, having seen it at all times of the day and night and in all seasons. I have watched the morning mist in summer evaporating in silvery-pink light with the warmth of dawn revealing the slowly gliding water. I have seen the autumn fog so thick as to render the opposite bank invisible, with carpets of leaves from the tall London plane trees silencing my steps as I walked on the footways of history and hope.

So many human narratives have been written here, on the banks of this river. Many tales have unfolded, some truth and some lies, but behind them all, the river and the land are always real. Around eleven thousand years ago, the landscape where the Embankment now hugs the margins of the River Thames was very different from how it looks today. It was altering dramatically. It had been locked in the grip of an Ice Age but the ice was receding. The terrain was warming and shifting slowly from being one of ice tundra towards vast marshes. Young water courses developed where previously there had been snow. Now water could flow freely and as it sought pathways to the sea it began to carve new rivers through the new wetlands. Flowing water attracts game and with it the predators, which in this and many other locations included early humans. The requirement to follow herds of game for food as they travelled was eased in the presence of any location that the game could readily be relied upon to visit.

It provided all key features of the triangle of life with the added advantages of fuel sources and defensibility. Access to unfrozen water provided by these new rivers improved the chances of survival for groups of humans and among these vast, whispering reed beds, the beginnings of early settled communities first began to form.

Through time, the strongest of the rivers merged together and one of these eventually became the Thames. River names still flow through daily conversation in the form of place names. Fleet Street, Effra Road, Bayswater, Wandsworth, Holborn. Today the rivers are mostly hidden. Along the streets where they flowed, there are not herds of game but herds of people, flooding daily in pursuit not of wild food and water but of money and entertainment, hunting not for game but for sandwiches and lattes on rushed lunch breaks.

In these vast marshes, the shifting landscape offered one more thing of significance to the people who were beginning to make it their home. The open sky joined with water and land in a space where rivers met the sea. The land, air and water joined with fire every time the sun rose and set. It gave a meeting point of planes, and elements. Rarely, even in nature, can all of these be seen unhindered and unobstructed across the horizon's span.

People who lived their lives in close proximity to the wild could not escape the constant need for information about changes in their environment. Changes in light, movements of birds, patterns of clouds and scents on the breeze all gave vital clues that were not merely a curiosity to be observed as we regard them today, if we do so at all, but were essential to survival. A place such as this where land, sea, air, sun and moon all met would have been auspicious beyond measure for the degree of awareness it afforded. These are places we understand from within ourselves, for their clear meeting of elemental forces. without any additional layers of cultural or religious meaning.

Now city life rushes past, for the most part oblivious to the history beneath it… and the real trouble with being oblivious to history is that if we are unaware of the clues it offers then we cannot truly follow an informed direction because we can't tell if we are going around in circles. The people living in that rush are functioning in a different layer of existence now for their survival. At one time, life here required people to be able to establish the triangle of life for themselves. Gradually, we built better shelters and became more consistently able to obtain water and food.

Now we seem to be regressing in our capabilities. What passes for living successfully in this environment means functioning ever more deeply in a virtual world. Many of us spend our days moving things around that will never have a physical form, between people we will never meet, to make money we will never see and which is no more than a promise made by people we don't know, to pay for being in homes which we will never own.

Perhaps there is nothing wrong with doing so but I believe that becoming so engrossed in the virtual world that we alter our perception of reality is inherently dangerous. We have created a world in which the unreal has real effect. People take actions based upon the online word of others who they have never even met. Handing away their will until they allow themselves to become willing to buy, change direction, harm, even destroy, all based upon nothing more than things that they were told in a virtual space.

One of the most real effects of all is how we feel. The virtual world has become a drug. A soporific trance from which we are becoming ever more unable to rouse ourselves and all the time, behind it, reality is watching us, drifting in the wind, shifting in the sky. 'Real' is in the eyes of birds and the quiet river, slipping past the stony bank and shining mud, wet, gleaming and grey. Real is in the morning fog and the sunlight that burns it away. Every now and then it nudges us to search for it. Scratching at the edge of our awareness like a half-heard sound that makes us momentarily look up from a daydream.

Chapter 11
Margins

Even the tiniest moments can be powerful. There are moments when the inner nomad insists on change and we just know we have to leave, wherever and whatever we were.

Nothing was working out. I felt like screaming. I needed to escape, couldn't stay in the trap of the un-wild. My time was vanishing like smoke on the wind. I had started out thinking I just needed to arrange a house move but it was so much more than that. "I need so much more time," I begged the Universe. "Throw it away then!" the Universe replied. "I don't understand. That doesn't make sense," babbled my fears. "Why would I throw away what I want more of?"

"Because it isn't real!" came the calm answer and suddenly I understood. We become trapped by the illusion of what we think we need. Throw it away and we spring the trap. Choices were converging to a vanishing point in front of me. Stay and keep the life I had before. Or let the house sale complete, jump and go, into the unknown. It might have made more sense to back out of the sale and wait, but I felt stifled by a quicksand of unreality, from which it was imperative that I claw my way free.

I had found a house and engaged a solicitor, but the seller wasn't answering any of the usual questions. The solicitor was ineffectual and it had dragged on for endless weeks. In the end, suspicion spilled over and I insisted the solicitor buck up and get some answers. It transpired that the drainage to a shared septic tank was a mess. The tank was on neighbouring farmland, subject to a rental agreement which it turned out was disputed by the farmer and the whole situation would take tens of thousands of pounds in remedial drainage work plus a lot more in legal fees to put right.

I pulled out, after having wasted a lot of time and money. It was the only thing I could sensibly do. I found another place, agreed a price and then two days later the vendor took it off the market, suddenly deciding that he didn't want to sell it any longer. I started again. I found a third place. In my heart I already knew it wasn't right. I was just going through the motions.

It was starting to feel weirdly unimportant. A new kind of feeling was rising within me. Not an emotion but a *way* of feeling. A new foundation upon which all other knowings took on new meaning. I had to go! The realisation was beating at me. "Go!" commanded the inner nomad. "You know the way. Just leave!" An idea was forming in the midst of all the fog. *Return to Cornwall!* I couldn't shake off the idea of heading back there for a few weeks while the purchase of the house progressed. "Third time lucky!" I told myself, though inside I didn't feel hopeful or lucky. Cornwall, on the other hand, lifted my heart and I breathed deeper every time I thought of it. All my practicality was getting me nowhere, so maybe it was time to try something impractical for a change.

Cornwall had exerted a magnetic pull on me since the first time I went there. I always felt drawn back to it after I had been gone awhile. Sometimes as soon as I left. On the Lizard, in the far south-west, the sea speaks with a unique and ever-present voice. Wherever I went, eventually it would seep slowly in from the background of my mind, creeping from the half-seen edges. Now it called to me in earnest. A strange soundless sound, resonant and powerful, flowed from that land and always seemed to find me wherever I went, calling me back. On the slim chance that friends I used to book a holiday rental with some years earlier were still there, I called and gratefully arranged to stay for one month, while it was empty, out of season. I thought I wouldn't need much longer than that.

In the long, dark cold of February, Monty and I got in the car and headed south. Our long journey began. With every mile that passed, the horizon opened up again, both in front of us and in my mind. Sometimes misty, sometimes clear. It felt like a heavy cloud was lifting from within me, taking the tension from the backs of my shoulders.

Evaporating quietly into the distance to that place where all things go which weighed us down until we discovered that they weren't real. I was starting to escape the illusion.

The horizon has a magic all its own. It holds a special relationship with human awareness. The ancient nomadic heritage of humankind still courses through our DNA. It nudges us from the deep recesses of our genes and compels us not only to keep moving, but also to ensure that we understand how to move onwards if we need to.

To the nomad, the horizon is vital, providing points of navigation, possible discoveries and the constant question of what is approaching. Watch the horizon and we have answers to all these things. The horizon is the ultimate 'in between' place, showing us our journey wherever we are going. If we lose sight of it for too long and see only what is around our feet, we lose our sense of direction.

Mostly, we no longer live nomadic lifestyles, but our DNA doesn't know that. For far longer than our recent lifestyle developments, our DNA has been there in the background. We are directed by it far more than we are by new technologies. The whispering wild resonates there and in the deep parts of our brains, yet we pay it less heed.

For century upon century, journeys have become layered into human experience. The necessity of surviving in the wild and on the move has taught us to pay deep attention to subtle cues all around us, not just to obvious spots but especially to the places where landscape was just changing a little. The margins, the in-between locations and most importantly what was in them. Plants, footprints, tracks? Which way were the trees leaning? Was there increasing or lessening water? Was it frozen or wet? These clues have long held great value on our journeys; helping us find routes and food sources and they still beckon our attention.

The myriad roadsides and verges of the UK and more widely into Europe hold many items. Some lost accidentally and others not just cast aside but deliberately left as offerings to whatever deities, protective spirits or other watchful guardians of wayfarers their owners believed in. Who knows what hopes they whispered and what journeys they made?

Is it any wonder that we have come to attach almost mystical significance to roads? Or that some of them seem imbued with the imprint of our lives? They have an air of philosophical mystique which is sometimes emphasised for those who spend more time on them. Long ago, the land that became the United Kingdom was home to people who placed items of value, apparently offerings, in locations such as lakes, rivers, bogs. It would be logical to imagine that they may also have done so around the coast but that those items are now long gone, carried away by the tide.

This group of islands are now known as the British Isles, but once they weren't islands at all. Low terrain linked this area to what is now called Europe. A link that reached into the Atlantic, connecting to Brittany in the south and stretched upwards to the north and east almost as far as Norway, divided from the great ice sheet only by the depths of the Norwegian Trench. The margins of the land have moved, many times and when we stand around the coast of the British Isles, there are many lost places, now out of reach to us, under the waves. It is only perception which makes us regard our current land edges as permanent.

I am always drawn to the coast. I only feel at home once I reach the edges and margins of this land that I was raised in. I am never quite comfortable until I have gone to the furthest extremity that land affords me. I can't seem to rest until I am within sight of the sea. Do our genes carry some sort of imprinted memory? This response isn't something I've learned. I didn't grow up by the sea or hear childhood stories of it. There were no seafarers among my relatives. It's just there. Stronger than conscious recall. A sort of inbuilt need to be at what feels like the edge of the physical world. Am I pulled by some sort of innate memory or other imprint to a land which now exists only underwater? Or is it that my soul recalls the distant reaches of some other land?

It feels like a reminder of somewhere else just out of reach. An echo of an echo. A somewhere that always feels nearer when I'm watching the ocean. An inexplicable sort of homing instinct which never quite resolves itself but only becomes partially satisfied when I am as close to the sea as I can get. What is Home? Disturbingly, I found I didn't know.

Monty and I went looking for it together. I wanted somewhere to live where I didn't feel trapped. Somewhere where we could go outside and not be enclosed by fences, walls and roads at every turn. Somewhere I could walk with Monty without coming up against boundaries every few minutes. So, although we needed somewhere to live, our search for home was becoming a search for the wild. That in turn came to describe a deeper search for the renewal of life, soul, purpose, identity. Reality.

Where is the wild? Perhaps it can be found in national parks and suchlike but by giving it defined areas are we not segregating it and increasing our separation? Just like when indigenous peoples were forced to live on reservations by people who only believed in owning and buying. Conveniently contained. Of course, it needs protecting but why can we not welcome it back among us? Our relationship to the wild cannot be formed on a transactional basis. Where is it in our daily lives? I had been crying out for it inside since the childhood days I left the first tussocks of grass behind. Wherever I go, wherever I live, after a while, that echo calls me back and I have to return. It is not just idly missing somewhere I enjoyed visiting, it is a visceral, compelling, enduring need.

Part 3
The Lost Lands

"Exploration is wired into our brains. If we can see the horizon, we want to know what's beyond."

Buzz Aldrin

Chapter 12
The Edge of Land

I was becoming an accidental nomad. Startling as this realisation was at first, when I thought about it, it didn't seem strange. That knowledge shattered complacency of belief, yet there was a rightness to it. We are all part nomad inside. Descended from the ancestral heritage of people for whom movement was a way of life. All grown from the same roots, like a tree with many branches. I thought at first that I didn't know what I was doing, but I found that actually there was a very strong part of me that did. I relished it. I cherished it. Rather than suppressing that voice as an irritating restlessness I began to treasure it.

My inner nomad began to speak loud and clear once I gave it the space to be heard. It called from the hedges and the sky. It emerged from the tiny trails where half-seen tracks led into the undergrowth. It peeked from behind cloud edges with the golden glint of sunshine. The inner nomad knew me better than I knew myself. As we headed southbound to Cornwall it grew stronger with every passing mile and minute. As did I. It was a relief to travel that road again. A watershed in which I knew that wherever the road took me, I would not be returning to my old life.

It had become evident that more than everything else, such as finding a home, I was really setting out to fulfil the ache to rediscover the horizon. I had become un-wild through the years and I knew of no more powerful place to experience the horizon than the Cornish coast. I first discovered it in my twenties and having done so I went back at any given opportunity. On the Lizard Peninsula, in the far south, I have always experienced the most powerful sense of connection to a place that I have ever known anywhere, including all the places that were my physical home at various times.

Crossing Wiltshire, heading up the long, steady incline onto Salisbury plain, I spotted a large layby just before reaching Stonehenge, and pulled over. The whole landscape was speaking. The road ahead beckoned and Cornwall called to me from far away. The sun had already risen and the sky was shifting from pale lavender to turquoise blue. The horizon, just above me, was an expanse of bright green, stretching along the entire skyline.

A chestnut brown kestrel hovered at the edge of field and road. Wings divided seconds with a rapid tempo, marked out with the beat of feathers against the endless space above. Visitors here inevitably seem to gravitate to the henge but those monumental sarsens sit against a wider background. There was something much older and wilder unfolding here in the landscape.

Everything to do with finding a house kept going wrong. But as I paused there and stopped to wonder, I realised it felt inexplicably right. I was scared but it was liberating. Refreshing even. I could feel old, worn-out mental barriers fading away like thawing ice. The world they had defined seemed to be dissolving away. So, I let things keep happening the way they were. The more I let go the more I knew it was right to do so.

Why could life not be simple? The way it was when people built that magnificent henge. If you needed somewhere to live, you found a suitable location that you liked and built a shelter there. Perhaps as part of a larger community of others, or maybe not. Everyone accepted that you could because everyone else did the same. You built it with the skills and materials available to you. There was no need to own anything. Just you and your relationship to the land.

There was no such thing as homelessness in times when people were allowed to make their own homes from whatever they could. The concept of buying or renting land was non-existent. No permission was necessary. Power could not be exerted by one human over another upon the basis of land possession before people thought of owning it.

Human and dog protected each other and there was no one to say where they may or may not go, or live.

Now, here we were, human and dog, trying to fight our way out of a maze of fences and boundaries, everywhere we turned, to be allowed just the simple space to breathe and live together. The words of Chief Seattle in 1854 were reverberating through my days and nights, "We do not own the land." The forget-me-not sky stretched above our heads.

A breeze blew out of the south. "Why do you humans want to keep limiting the unlimited?" it asked. "Does it scare you so much?" I drank in the air, trying to fill myself with this morning so it might live in every moment of my life. We continued on, skirting around the urban obstacle of Exeter as quickly as possible, escaping onto the A30 over Bodmin. Rugged and mysterious Bodmin, the last real high ground on our journey. A buzzard circled over the field next to the road, broad wings stroking the wind with fingery feathers.

Bodmin feels like the last geographical hurdle to cross before heading down from the moors towards Helston and the distant southwest. From there I pointed the car south on the last leg of the journey, with mounting excitement and relief. Every time I return to the Lizard, when I get past Helston and start to draw closer, I always have a tide-strong sense of being in a place which is different from anywhere else.

B3297 seems like a funny thing to call a road which carries us through such a mystical landscape. After Helston, it becomes a curving, winding twist of grey leading into the vanishing point where it feels like land, sky and sea are all merging. Here I breathe more easily. It brings an intense relief and always the same feeling of extreme homecoming. Leaving to go back to wherever was my geographical home always felt like going away to somewhere that was just any other place.

The coastline at this southern extremity is the strongest example of the power of a 'margin' or joining place that I have so far encountered. Am I only at home in the in-between places? Am I even seeking somewhere out there which no longer exists upon solid land? Lost to all but genetic memory in the farthest reaches of our history? This time, when I sought the shimmering clifftops where drifts of flowers sprawled, suspended above the sea by translucent rock, it was with my new friend at my side.

With Monty for a travelling companion and not a lot that I was sure of other than the fact of his massive importance to me, I stepped into the unknown. Unhesitatingly, Monty came too.

It felt like I was melting around the edges, dissolving into a shared experience with my dog and the road ahead. The hardened constraints of expectation were melting. Whose expectations were they anyway? Not mine. Not Monty's. Together we fused with each other and the land. We weren't so much making a journey as falling into a different awareness. One which had always been there but which I had somehow pushed aside and been in danger of forgetting more profoundly.

On many roadsides and in many weathers, we had made stops on our search. Each time we moved on we stepped into the in-between spaces a little more and I started to sense their voices with increasing strength. I started to actively seek them and what they could teach me.

On the edges of the roads where I stopped with Monty, I looked more closely at what was happening there. At first whether I could get him safely out of the car and onto a grass verge, but then it became automatic to look at what was on the verge. Was there litter or was it uncontaminated? Was there space to walk away from the road, among trees or into a field? Or was it merely a tightly hemmed strip of green squeezed between tarmac boundaries? Was it tethered by metal and wire boundaries or could it breathe?

The regular stops needed by a young dog on a long journey introduced new considerations for me on the road. Water stops and toilet stops were now as essential as fuel. I have always enjoyed driving long- distance car journeys but previously I had an instinctive dislike of breaking the journey more than absolutely necessary, preferring instead to keep moving.

With Monty, my parameters for what was necessary suddenly shifted. The all-important search for a patch of grass every couple of hours, in proximity to a safe place to pull over, had become a vital consideration of any journey. This meant discovering an array of petrol stations, laybys and undefinable roadside stopping points which I would never be able to find a second time. Their very transience became their defining characteristic, whispering of journeys made and yet to come. The companionship and shared understanding of human and dog on the road.

Narrow, ambiguous spots along the way which previously have gone unnoticed as just the backdrop of a journey to somewhere else. Now I found my feet coming into contact with them. Random locations, where the wild still tries to clutch at its existence around the perimeter of our rush and crush while we whizz by on our way to somewhere else.

Sometimes, standing there in one of those margins, I would watch cars hurtling past. I remembered Oak Tree in the lane I had left behind and wondered, 'Can they even see me?' Or once I stepped into the margins, had I somehow stepped off the page of their world and become invisible to everyone in it? Perhaps there are some words which, like an incantation, make us fade from the sight of others. Is 'homeless' one of them? Sure, I wanted a home of my own, but I liked this state of vanishing. Of invisibility from the un-wild and un-real. I didn't want to return to the non-world.

With each gust of wind, the road and the wild, resurgent and vibrant, crept back from the edges. No longer like a stranger just pushed to the fringes but more a valid state of being that was my right and my heritage as a human. Not just an accident of experience. I was remembering something else. Something older.

Perhaps we are always marginal. We came from a world that had fewer false definitions. Maybe in our current cultures we are hanging on to fixed, defined locations like a lifeline to an inadequate but familiar map that we have convinced ourselves is real, when really, we are part of the tide of some larger world.

Spots of rain fell onto the warm earth, dropping through the in-between spaces in my awareness. My remaining mind stirred and flexed at their touch, the sense of in-betweenness expanding, with the faintest memories of how things used to feel when I was very young. What are these margins that go unnoticed but link everywhere together? Almost like the dark matter of the Universe, binding the seen and unseen worlds.

Chapter 13
The High Place

On the Lizard cliffs, the land, sea and sky meet up in a way that is utterly breathtaking. I didn't need anything to be there other than what nature had put there. There was always something about it that was hard to explain. I've never needed it to be anything other than what it was. I just wanted to look at it; breathe it in and listen to the sea until I could feel the pulse of it against the rocks in the cells of my own body and echoing in my dreams.

As long as the sun came up and went down, the wind blew on my face, the ancient rocks faced out to sea as they had done for thousands of years and the fog gathered in the evenings, it was perfect being exactly itself, how it was meant to be. I went because of the Places I knew there that called me back. If I stayed away too long, I missed them, like old friends.

One of these is so alive with energy that the whole atmosphere there seems to be constantly trembling, giving it an air of semi-transparency. A rocky trail of red serpentine, about a mile long, leads out to the coastal path. Tussocky fields and a broad swathe of grass stretch away from a narrow trail separated by a sturdy gate from the enormous cliffs. Giant, weather-battered slabs of granite mark the edge of the land, where it gives way to the beginning of the world of water. The green and blue tide surges endlessly around their feet and the breeze is an airy spirit of freshness and change. There at this joining point is the Place.

One rocky outcropping, neither the biggest nor the highest, is topped by exposed, element-carved rocks into a shape like the head of a griffin-type being, deep-eyed and fiercely staring, complete with the front of its chest emerging from the cliff-edge and two front paws, pointing towards the waves. Between its paws a natural hollow on the seaward side is sheltered from all but the most directly facing of winds.

An ancient watcher, the rock-being gazes out to sea. Memories of ages have washed over it, the lives of many people have begun and passed through this land and these waters. It has gazed while all the turns of our human histories, across the long centuries, have unfolded. Lichen gives it a marbling camouflage of tawny orange-browns and greens. Flowers spread around its paws, tumbling over its back.

Here, everything is intensified. Timelessness is tangible, like something that can be inhaled with the sea-spray. It can be tasted. The light has such power here that it seems it is not the light but the physical world that is translucent. The force of light on sea and sky is so strong that they appear to merge completely, leaving only a mysterious bright void. A portal to other, brighter worlds. The solid rock of cliffs facing along the edge of land appears thin, almost dematerialising in the brilliance while the doorway of light gains in strength.

As soon as I got back to the village, from being away, I could never get out onto the coast path fast enough. I wanted to spend my life there, many lifetimes, staring out to sea like the rock-being. I wanted to sit between its paws and become one with the cliffs. Watching the light change, hearing the singing breeze breathing all around me and feeling the low, soft roar of the ocean filling my being until I pulsed with it to my core, like the land itself.

It should not have surprised me then, that I would find myself pulled back there. Or that I would head for that extreme edge of the rugged coast as fast as I could. True to my nature, not happy until I was up against the edge of the sea, as far south as I could go without getting my feet wet. This time I couldn't wait to bring Monty here to this southernmost extremity and get him out onto that path. I needed to get him here. To bring him to this Place. Whether to connect him to it or the two parts of my life together, I wasn't sure.

We stayed at the house I had rented many times before. Tall and white, with thick stone walls, it sits solidly at the top of the lane down to Caerthillian Cove, with no passing cars. An air of calmness pervades its view. My mother and I, called by the same mutual need for return, used to come here, summer and winter alike. The singing sea permeates the air here in all directions, merging waking and dream-state together in one seamless fusion of something like timelessness, but different.

In wet weather the fog siren called longingly from the lighthouse. The bedroom overlooked the sea through a large bay window that made it feel like being outside. I could hear the sea's voice in my sleep. A bit like sleeping on the deck of a boat, but drier. All the ancient seafaring history, playing out across time on the tapestry of waves. Never static. Never stopping. With the curtains left open, the distant lights of ships passed slowly by. The sense of constant motion permeated everything. I could feel myself becoming porous to this landscape, absorbing it on some unseen level. Becoming space. Energy.

As soon as morning light broke the darkness, I headed out with Monty into the lane. The air was edgy with a hard bite of ice seldom brought by winter this far south. It spoke of challenge, uttering the warning not to underestimate the wild, even here in this mild land. The darkness was brooding. The land felt watchful. Everything felt touched with tension like static electricity.

Our trail led over the small headland and down the curving side of the cliff, towards a small stream of clear, fresh water, tumbling through a narrow ravine, lush with greenery and racing to fall into the sea. Monty ran up to it, but stopped short of putting his paws in, jumped towards it again and padded around it a bit, looking excited but uncertain. I realised he had never seen running water in a swift-flowing stream like this before. *He's only ever seen water in a bowl, or rain on the ground*, I mused. *He's waiting to see what I do.* Walking to the water's edge I squatted and let the clear water run over my fingers, saying to him, "Water. Water." Then cupped it in my hands and drank.

It was the freshest, coldest water I have ever tasted. It was exquisite. I would rather have drunk that than the most expensive offering in any restaurant on earth. Monty, immediately reassured, went straight to it, dabbled both his front paws in and drank thirstily. "Water," I told him again so that he would know the word. "It's good water." I took up a deep double handful, drank and splashed it on my face and head, then did it again. The temperature felt glacial. It was one of the most refreshing things I have ever done.

I needed that water, as if I had been dying of a deeper kind of thirst. I felt it renewing me with the touch of the wild. A cold, easterly breeze was stinging my wet eyelids. Instead of turning away, I faced the sea and looked into the breeze. To the eastern horizon, broad stripes of white light and deep shadow were stretching across the water. I stood with Monty on that narrow promontory that jutted out into infinity. Suddenly, here, we were no longer small, but a facet of all that was vast.

Chapter 14
Thunder and Snow

This place never compromises. It is wild to the core. Humans approach and hang on around the fringes, a few blithely, many haphazardly, some with reverence, like wanderers seeking shelter at the court of King Arthur. Just like that fabled seat, this place holds power. It turns no one away, but people seem to meet themselves here, as if something about it reflects the inner being.

Magnetically, it both attracts and repels. Just like travellers to a royal court, some come seeking sight of jewels, in the blue of the sea, the gold of the sun and glorious views for tales to impress their friends. Maybe they find it. Others set out but don't make it this far. They stop further north and say they've been to Cornwall, when all they have really done is just about cross the county boundary and travel a little way down the north Cornish coast. I have heard them declare this, in a 'ticked that off the list' kind of way. Wincing inside I smile politely.

Maybe you have, maybe you haven't. This place is different. It is not just Cornwall. It is Lys Ardh. You will either find it, or you won't. Even if you come here, you may not find it.

Nothing is still here. All is constant motion. Wind, waves, light, birds, clouds and rain. Always moving. Maybe it is because of this, that suddenly the stillness at the centre of all the motion in the Universe, becomes clearer here.

The light was intensifying and polarising in every direction. The colours of sea and sky deepening to a level of drama which was unusual even for here. Threads of pure indigo shadow and vibrant white light spanned the panorama of the sea, met by a deep, slate-grey sky, shot with silvery fire. Stunned by the intensity, I stood on the upper curve of the headland, staring, as the lines of light and shadow narrowed and intensified, moving over the sea. Until something on the wind told me, "Go! It is time to go!" I don't know what spoke. Voice of the wild? Voice of the sea? I left as soon as I heard it, though I could not have given it a name. Perhaps it was some deep knowledge of my inner nomad. Calling Monty to me I headed back up the path, hugging the line of the dry-stone wall. Just as I reached the gate, a clap of thunder boomed overhead, rumbling a deep warning.

In moments the sky had gone from morning light to near-dusk in appearance. Thunder was growling over the sea. Out of an illogical darkness which gripped the land, snowflakes came whirling past, thickly bejewelling Monty's velvet ebon fur with sparkling stars.

Amid this surreal scene, as we passed through the gate, Monty paused at the side of the lane, glossy, jet-coloured and warm, covered in twinkling white sparkles of ice. That image of him in the wild is graven in my brain. Sometimes he seemed half puppy, half young wolf. I glanced back along the headland towards the sea and as I did so a massive rainbow sprang into view and leaped dazzlingly across the clear gap between the expanse of looming clouds.

The unexpected snow hardened into hail, flung at us by a strengthening wind. Snow was now encrusting the grass and old bracken at the side of the lane and the hailstones were peppering us like small bullets. They were stinging my face and must have been doing the same to Monty's nose. He looked at me with a perplexed expression. "Go quickly!" I told him and ran with him as he raced back up the slippery, uneven lane towards the shelter of the house that I wished we could call home.

I needed to be as close as possible to this path, to live where this little ribbon of reality weaves its way through the fabric of the Universe like some sort of timeless walkway through the stars. A magical spot in the Infinite.

Every day, Monty and I walked to the meeting points of land, sea and sky, wandering along the margins of the solid world. Celandines and violets studded the grass above Caerthillian Cove. Thick, wet bracken soaked my shoes as I climbed up out of the gulley crossing the little footbridge and up the rising eastbound track.

Smells of earth and ozone filled every breath. The tiny acts of rediscovering our connection to the wild were a pleasure of sharing life with Monty. An adventure of noticing and observing. When I worried, he played. I asked him questions and taking his advice, cast worry away. It evaporated on the sea breeze, like mist. He jumped up on the rough stone wall. Stressed about getting back, I crossly ordered him to get down and come with me. Then checked myself and reined in my impatience. What was I in such a rush for anyway? Would it matter if I took ten minutes longer?

I stopped and stroked him. He looked at me puppyishly and then turned his face to the breeze, looking out to sea with the wisdom of millennia engraved into his expression. "What are you doing up here, Monty?" I asked him. "Come try it and see for yourself," the little wag of his tail invited me. I pulled myself up beside him and sat on the ancient wall.

From there it was obvious. The view of the sea and surrounding land was clearer. The breeze he was sniffing was laden with the scents of rain, the vegetation and earth. Each element distinct as the notes in a piece of music, separate but linked. As I inhaled, I savoured it like he seemed to, finding that by letting the air drift slowly across the backs of my nostrils, not merely breathing in and out like a robot, I could easily distinguish the different aromas.

Sudden images arose in my mind from the multi-layered scents. *Is this what it is like for a dog? Clear mental imagery, based upon their experiences, unfolding direct and untainted by judgement or opinion?* It felt like drinking from the stream of life itself. I made notes for books without trying to direct or control the outcomes. Monty made me laugh. He brought constant joy. Every time I worried, he responded with love and fun. I wrote about our conversations. I sketched him in all sorts of situations. On the wall, on the cliffs looking at the sea, jumping up and down playfully.

The notes naturally evolved into a manuscript and very soon, I'd written my first book. It grew from our relationship with each other. I called it *Conversations with my Dog* because that's what it was. As I watched how he lived I knew wordlessly what he would write if he could. He expressed Montyness and I wrote it into words for us both. I started placing drawings with text, aiming to encapsulate the same spirit of fun and freedom that Monty exuded in every playful, loving wag of his tail.

With every page-turn of the passing moments here, the sea calls me. As it always has. Sweeping through me with a tide much stronger than just memories of holidays or dreams of far-off lands. A ceaseless reverberation echoes from within. Is it the sea itself that exerts such a pull on my soul? Or is it something else? Something across the sea, under, or within it? Only here, on the Lizard, does it have the power to make me feel like I am dissolving into some larger world. Even the cliffs have a semi-transparency, as though they exist half in this world and half somewhere else. Though huge, sometimes they seem ethereal.

"What's solid?" I heard Robin, who I loved and who died years earlier asking me from our memories. "That rock you call solid is mostly made of empty space," he used to say to me. "The space between the particles of an atom is vast. So physical things like the rocks, the cliffs, even our own bodies are still about 99.9% 'nothing.' Whatever that is. We still aren't really sure. What keeps things separate is that the bits of the atoms which are there are arranged differently from each other. That's why some things can merge with each other and some can't."

"It's all perception," murmured the tide. Skylarks danced through the air, warbling melodious counterpoints to the sonorous tide. "It's all perception," whispered the sky. "Perception," echoed the distant grey line of Land's End faintly scoring the boundary between sea and sky in the west, fading and then emerging from the mist. Perception, perception…

Years before, I had casually mentioned at work that I was going away for a week to Cornwall. I had already been there a couple of times that year, but for me that was normal. When a colleague asked me, "What's there?" I found it a slightly odd question but I meant it quite literally when I replied, "Nothing."

There are lots of things in Cornwall but I was trying to convey that I wasn't going there for urban activities, shops or any physical object, rather for the sheer, wonderful, lack of things. I went for the fact that it was wild. It was things and the widespread obsession with them that I sought to leave behind. In fact, in Lizard village there was hardly any mobile phone signal on most networks, which suited me fine. Unless you stood at an exact point on the village green and faced in a specific direction, mobile phone reception was all but non-existent. It was wonderful! Walk six feet in any direction from that spot and the signal wavered. Two more and it disappeared completely. The only other option, strangely, was to walk out to the coast path, to a particular outcropping of rock, on top of which there was also a strong signal, which once again vanished a few feet away.

My colleague paused, then said in a puzzled tone of voice, "Oh." Then after a second, "We thought maybe you had a man there?" Bemused, all I could reply was, "Why…?" To which he pointed out that because I kept going back, the team had assumed I was seeing someone there. My patient explanation that it wasn't a person I was going back there for but the lack of people, was met with a hint of disappointed scepticism. I couldn't help pondering why knowing that I enjoyed returning to a location was automatically equated to a personal human relationship. Could I not just go somewhere because I liked it?

Now I had come back here because of need. This place felt vital to me. I needed the icy water, the singing wind and the rhythmic sea. The patterns of light here had become essential. The wild was essential too and nowhere was I more connected to it than here.

Chapter 15
What is 'Wild'?

Wild is a word that can be used to mean many things. The usage of words can change through time. Wild is by nature hard to define. It wouldn't be wild if we could put a cage of limitation around it since all description is limiting. According to the Cambridge dictionary the word 'wild' means "uncontrolled, violent or extreme." Yet many things are truly wild, without any of those descriptions applying to them. A newly hatched hawk chick is none of these things, yet its heart is completely wild. The word can even be interpreted as freaky or outlandish but before it came to mean any of these things, I think in the simplest sense it literally meant 'not tamed'.

Wild is the voice of the wind, falling from high ground, untrammelled by wires and walls. Wild is the taste of cold rainwater that has rushed across rock and filtered through reeds. Ancient as the stars, new as a bird's egg in springtime. Wild is the untamed world. Wild was stirring on the wind, in the reeds, in the deep sky above. It stirred within me. It shone in my dog's eyes, resonant and true. Rushing swiftly across the sea with the gathering dawn, touching the wings of the skylarks streaming upwards towards the sky in the gathering light.

Wild is whole, wild is real. It is ourselves, complete, before we try to remove the parts of our consciousness which lifestyles convince us to leave behind. The wild is vanishing from our world and it had been vanishing from me, slowly, subtly, while I wasn't paying attention and looked at other things. I vowed to reclaim it with both hands. I held onto it like holding onto breath itself.

In the wild places is born our sense of connectedness to life. Without that link we are restricted in the full use of our natural abilities. When we are unable to direct these as nature intended them to be used, we are diminished. Mentally, physically, spiritually.

Uneasiness arises in that limitation, one which is hard to pin down or sometimes even recognise. Our ancient selves step forth from forgotten places, so we label them as dark or primitive and start to fear ourselves. We try to drown our senses out by chattering online, buying things, or distracting ourselves with entertainments. But they remain, still, whispering in the parts of our minds we have forgotten, about our larger selves. We have thought that we could live without many things; without hunting, without watching the sky for changes in the weather and perhaps we can, but we cannot live without ourselves. Without the parts of us we left behind.

These are the moments when the wild world speaks to us, sometimes directly or at others through its inhabitants, a bird, animal, or tree, even a pebble. I've always picked up stones, feathers and other small things, as I guess most children do. Now I made a determined effort to do all these things again that we do instinctively when young. I held a shell and asked what my younger self used to do.

Slowly an awakening memory curled up from its deep resting place. It was more about reaching out with self than with physical sight to look for patterns. More like touching with the mind than the hands. A much fuller way of experiencing. Smaller hands, yet still my own, holding an oval white pebble, warmed by the sun, plucked from the pavement near my school. Words came from distantly above me: "Put that down! It's dirty!" I ignored them. The small stone was glowing pure white and hot from the summer's day, like snow on fire. One of the cleanest things I have ever seen. I was enthralled that something so white could come from the brown earth.

There is spirit in all wild things. Children know this. They don't separate themselves from it. They reach out with all senses available to them, curious, unhindered by expectation and receive what comes back without judgement. Now I would hang onto my right to reclaim that connection as tightly as the younger me held onto that stone.

Wild does not mean unsafe. It does not mean primitive or backward. It does not have to be violent, uncontrolled, or extreme. It can mean attuned, original, untainted. Ignoring 'wild' can be much more unsafe than heeding it. In fact, failing to observe it can be downright perilous at times. Silent agreement whispers through the centuries from our ancestral occupants of the drowned lands that once surrounded these green, rocky islands, long ago.

Wild is not a dirty word. Wild is vital. Wild is us. But we can't sense the wild if our brains are clogged up with clutter and the nonsense of the unreal. Wild does not compromise, nor does it seek permission to be. It doesn't care what you or I think about it. Wild can draw us to a place or drive us from it. It had pulled me back here to this exact spot from the very first time I set foot here. But what did that mean for me? Wild does not need money or things. It simply is. If a hawk wants to raise young it makes a nest. A fox makes a den. Wild things seek no permission either to move or to make a home, they just do.

Chapter 16
The Lost Lands

The third prospective house move I had planned to make also went wrong. I knew by now that I hadn't really wanted it to succeed. It was just another place to get trapped. I was kidding myself. My heart wasn't there. It was here, on the Lizard. But I now had nowhere to live. I moved from one temporary arrangement to another.

The more I searched for a home, the more I came to understand that finding the way home means paying attention to the route we are taking and what it can tell us. Monty made me notice details about my surroundings. *What's important?* I started to ask. *What really matters to me?* Monty was obviously wiser than me, so I asked him too. "Hey, Monty?" I enquired as we meandered along the trail to the headland above Caerthillian Cove. "Where are we going to live?" He looked round at me with his ears blowing in the breeze. In his eyes full of love, the answer needed no words to express it. "Together!" he replied without words.

"But we need a home."

"My home is where you are," he replied with a soft wag of his tail.

"I'm glad."

It was only later I was to realise that rather than having nowhere to go, as I had thought, rather I had everywhere to go. All I had to do was choose a direction. I was in between homes, in between locations. I was truly becoming marginal. But I was growing. I had started noticing the margins and somehow seemed to have fallen into them. Or perhaps they had expanded and surrounded me. Maybe they had always been there, unnoticed, and there were more of them than

I thought.

It was starkly obvious that I had been trying to buy in the wrong location. Despite the fact that I had wanted to live in Cornwall since the first time I ever went there, a home there felt like something I couldn't have. Too expensive, too unattainable, too much the province of rich second home-owners. The High Place, so dear to me, was out of my reach. I had searched everywhere else, for places which reminded me of Cornwall, so that I could feel close to it. But all the reminders ever served to do was to make me want to leave them and go back. Still, my travels with Monty taught me a lot. Place names which might otherwise have been just words, became lived experiences, each with their own beauty. Each with something to teach.

Pembrokeshire on the Welsh coast bore a striking similarity to parts of Cornwall. There was something intangible about the shape of the terrain as it ran on the last, long stretch towards the sea that spoke to me of the south-western span of Cornish coast along the Lizard Peninsula and around to the west. It surprised me for a while, until I visualised how things used to be before the last Ice Age, when dry land extended around what is now the British Isles, far beyond the parameters of our current coastline. There are nuances to the appearance of the coastline in Cornwall that are not quite the same anywhere else.

Still the echoes in Pembrokeshire were strong enough to show that they were the remaining edges of a larger terrain which had been swallowed by the encroaching sea. While it might take a long time to drive round by road, if I imagined looking down from the viewpoint of a seagull, the actual distance across the waves between the two was surprisingly small. Scant wonder then that it should be similar when it would once have been part of the same expanse.

Doggerland, named after Dogger Bank, is what we now call the swathes of drowned land which were lost on the eastern side of the United Kingdom. Although it is anyone's guess how the people who once populated the hills and valleys of that land used to describe it. Migratory hunter-gatherers who moved with the seasons would certainly have had an acute sense of the geography that they covered. Anyone who roamed there then would not have been met with the sight of the ocean unless they wandered as far as the Norwegian Trench.

As the sea rose, by just a few feet each century, it compelled them inexorably towards higher ground. Slowly, the last of them were forced onto the highest ground that we now recognise as the countries which exist today. Now, the ocean covers their bones and tools. The stories of those lives have washed away. But they are still speaking to us, down the long span of history, and despite all our apparent differences we still face the same challenge they did.

The sea is still rising. Our coast is still changing. It knows more about us than we do. Those early nomads had physical access to great expanses of land that no longer exist above water. They walked where we no longer can. Their preserved footprints have been discovered in ancient mud, long since turned to stone on the sea-bed. The feet that once made them were going somewhere on a journey now long vanished into time. Those feet knew no boundaries, beyond what geography made physically unattainable to them. Not for them the cages of tarmac roads and wire, hemming in their path. Those unfettered feet wandered naturally upon ever unfolding ways. The wild was home for them, not something to be driven back and contained. They did not walk past small patches of green on the way to somewhere else, they lived within it and never knew the pain of such separation.

I'd heard of Doggerland, referring to the eastern coast, but it was the western similarities of Wales and Cornwall which now gave me pause for thought. Sea levels did not rise only in the east, but all around what is now the United Kingdom. In the west and to the south also, land must have vanished underwater. The coastlines of Pembrokeshire and Cornwall were once not coast at all but just the beginning of a larger stretch of land.

What other places also lost and since unnamed in our time, have vanished? What shores did people once venture to and stand gazing upon younger seas? They wandered through my dreams, those explorers from long ago. Straight out of time through the portals of dreaming. Whether the touch of ancestral spirits or some deeply imprinted genetic memory surfacing like whales from under the sea. I felt closer to them and closer to myself for the sense of their proximity.

Around the world, indigenous peoples have been aware of the importance of remembering their ancestors and honouring them. They believe our ancestors stay close and guide us. Maybe this is how our ancestors speak. In the voices of the wind and sea, singing their memories in our dreams. Maybe when we join them, we will speak through ripples on sand and the branches of trees, giving voice to our will and reaching out to those who listen.

It's strange how in Western cultures we use the term 'First nations' to refer to indigenous peoples where they are the earliest known inhabitants of a region. Or the earliest known to us. It is intended respectfully as an acknowledgement that their ways were here before ours. But speaking with them reveals a different story. They say that there were others before them. When will we listen?

The Ojibwe creation myth describes them as the second nations. It tells that the first nations as they perceived them were earlier and their civilisations were destroyed in a great flood. A theme which is echoed in many tribal creation stories all over planet Earth. If we could travel far back in time, to speak with those more ancient peoples, would they exclaim, "No, we weren't the first either! There was someone here before us too!" What then does that make us? Maybe third or fourth nations? Children certainly. Races with a lot to learn.

I felt alone. Dwarfed by the tide of ignorance which has swept through the intervening years of supposed progress, while we invented ever more things with which to separate ourselves from the wild. Decade upon decade of barriers and disconnection from the fullness of life. I faced the sky and sea, as the sweep of time and timelessness spoke of all the human stories gone before me. "Where are you, Ancestors?" I called into the gathering wind. The answer was immediate, barely had I formed the words. "Here!" they told me, forcefully. "Here."

I breathed in the sense of their presence. "We never left. It was you who stopped seeing and hearing us. We who are all around you, we never leave." There was something else, deeper, forming. "It is only your notion of leaving that separates us. Cast off these illusions that cloud your mind and see!" And I saw, just for an instant, but it was enough. Through the barrier, through the veil. To the bigger world. I sat by the ancient rock, the Watcher stone, comfortable between its paws, both sheltered and exposed. With my arms around Monty, I saw the inner land we lose sight of when we forget that we are wild and infinite beings.

The pulse of the land touched everything, the trails and flowers, the sweet air and the heart of the rock, Monty's heartbeat and mine. With the ancient one we watched the sea. Monty's brown eyes spoke love to eternity. Wise as the stones as he looked across the waves into the mist. His soft black feathery fur blew in the breeze and mingled with my brown hair. I pressed my face against his neck and breathed the scent of him, warm and clean. I looked at him in the way I had when he was a tiny puppy all sparkling with frost on that midwinter night. Seeing both detail and spirit. I let myself melt into the touch of his warmth and the song of the sea. The smell of salt filling our nostrils. Pulse of the ancient land beneath us. One. Human, dog and land.

But still, I was about to leave Cornwall and the Lys Ardh again.

Part 4

We Are Dreaming

"Reality is merely an illusion, albeit a very persistent one."

Albert Einstein

Chapter 17
Messenger

Once, long ago, I dreamed I was looking around a sunlit garden, not knowing quite why I was there. It reminded me of my mother's garden, with lush flowering bushes and magnificent tall roses as high as trees, reaching for the blue sky. The colours of the dream were as brilliant as any summer's day. Suddenly a tiny hoverfly darted into full view, vividly hanging suspended in the air in front of my face, just inches from my eyes, wings a shining storm of energy.

I looked straight at it and somehow the sight of it instantly caused me to know that I was dreaming. In that flash of gleaming wings, I became lucid, asleep and dreaming, but conscious in the dream-state. I woke up physically a second later, but the image stayed with me. Graven in gold on the flow of my thoughts. That tiny creature compellingly hovered in my consciousness, flitting into my waking mind, as it had into the dream. A miniature burnished messenger bidding me, "Wake up!"

Now Mum was gone. I had returned to the Cambridgeshire Fens as a matter of urgency. She was ill, not with disease, but just fading. Life was leaving her. Desolately, I thought that it was separation from the wild; the move into an artificial place and the lost hope of returning to Cornwall, which were taking a final toll on her strength. She was giving up. I had been back to visit before, seeing her start to weaken but hoping she would hold on.

I brought her all her favourite foods and left them packaged in small quantities ready for her to nibble on. She still had enthusiasm and enjoyment so I hoped that she might eat while I was away, not just while I was there. I plated her a lovely assortment of all her favourite tasty treats, salmon, ham and cheese. Easy to eat nibbles. Monty jumped up next to her on the bed and sat by her elbow while she ate. He made not the faintest move to try and take any scrap of food from her plate, although it must have smelled most enticing to him. He just sat there proudly, looking straight at me while I unpacked the shopping, as if to say "Don't you worry, I'll watch Nanna. You do what you need to. I will protect her!"

I just wanted her to rally and eat something, to hold on, but I feared that inside her the will to do so was evaporating. She couldn't tell me. Perhaps she couldn't even tell herself. Her strength was leaving her bit by bit. She was giving up on life. I should have taken her back to Cornwall years ago, when we had longed to find a way to live there. I should have found a way. Suddenly there is no more time for 'should.' No more chances. Only whatever we are left with at the end of all our decisions. The physical results start to fall away and all that is left is love and spirit.

It was becoming clear to me that I would never have time to find us the place together in Cornwall for which we had once hoped. It wasn't going to work out but I knew I had to do something. It seemed that if I was going to find somewhere for us both for a while I could do it more cost-effectively back in the Fens. Joy sparked across her face when I said I would find us a place somewhere else back out east and she could come and live with me again. Her eyes shone and her response, "Oh good!" rocked her whole body with the force of its emphasis. I still didn't recognise it but we were already running out of time more quickly than I thought.

I had returned to Cornwall just long enough to give up my rental. Once again, I packed up all my things into the car, Monty jumped in, and we headed off back to the Fens, not knowing that before long, they would never seem the same to me again and nor would anywhere else. When I arrived back, the brief show of strength she had made at my last visit had dissipated. She seemed to be getting thinner and more transparent somehow, less solid, as though she was dematerialising in front of my eyes. Monty sat next to her like before but unlike last time when he had just guarded her, now he was visibly agitated and pawed at her incessantly. He wouldn't calm down. Mum, who had always loved to stroke and tickle him, was pushing him away in distress.

Monty is a strong young dog and his considerate behaviour in the past had shown me that he knew how to be gentle with her frailty. But apparently, he also knows when people are ill and it upset him. The pawing was his way of trying to give warning to us to help. He wouldn't relax. I apologised to Mum, hurriedly took Monty away and came back without him.

"Monty?" she whispered.

"It's OK," I reassured her. "I left him with friends. He's fine."

"Oh, poor Monty," she replied.

I explained that I had left him with them because he kept bothering her. "He knows I'm dying," she stated, and the only way I could think to reply was to say equally matter-of-factly, "animals know these things." It wasn't intended to sound blunt or cold, just to give calm acknowledgement and recognition of her brave statement. She didn't need hysterics or emotion, she needed respect.

I went away, gathered a few personal items and came straight back with the intention of staying as long as I had to. No one quite knew how long she had. Dying, unless some accident befalls us, is a slow-ish process by which a person releases their hold on life and their connection to their body. We spend our whole lives doing our very best to remain attached to our bodies, so letting go and leaving them is challenging. It takes as long as it takes to stop fighting our conditioning and let go. I had no way of knowing how her process would unfold. Western culture largely alienates death, whether by over-medicalisation, ingrained religiosity, or just plain old fear, so I had very little substantial knowledge to enable me to act as her guide.

She was still eating occasional mouthfuls of food, no longer for nourishment, but for the sake of sharing and enjoying the human connection that it brings. She was weakening but still seemed to enjoy the idea of having whatever flavours she felt like. Why do we wait until dying before allowing ourselves to eat desserts at any time of day?

We ate soft cheesecake, with mango and vanilla ice cream. It was the last meal we shared together. It reminded me of all those times we had sat up late together watching silly films. Silently now, in unspoken wishes, we both longed for those days. They hung between us, suddenly as inaccessible now as the home we had left behind. She ate with difficulty, but gratefully, as though appreciating a sense of normality and still hoping somehow that things would return to how they once were. That we would go home and have more seasons and sunrises together. More ice creams, festive dinners and cups of hot coffee. She still smiled and spoke cheerfully, though barely above a whisper. "That was lovely," she murmured, and as I cleared away the plates, "What shall we do next?"

I couldn't answer. How do you tell someone who can barely stay awake that this will be the night they will drift into a sleep they will most likely not rise from? Her eyes were begging me to turn back the clock and make things how they had once been. My mind floundered when trying to come up with an answer in the face of that knowledge. My hesitant silence must have been answer enough for her. Although she didn't speak, I heard her thought reverberate through the space between us as if she had shouted aloud, *"Oh, next I die!"* We never know how it will happen, until finally we reach the point where we do. We just couldn't articulate the enormity of the moment before us. Me through lack of words and her because she hardly had the strength to form them.

"Don't go!" Her two simple words hit me with a universe full of meaning. She gripped me with her last strength as though hanging onto something more. What was it she was clutching? Life, love, the things left unsaid? I will never know.

Time runs out. There is a moment in all our relationships after which we get left only with questions. She seemed to be echoing the fears and loneliness of all the times I had left her before and she must have wanted to say those words, but never did. I had to go to work,

I always had to do something. Work was more important. But there is nothing more important and I knew that now, too late to say it. Suddenly there was too much to say. Too many things I needed to put right which I should have done long before. Resorting to the simplest words I could find I wrapped my arms around her and affirmed with every ounce of conviction I could find, "I'm going nowhere!"

I slept by her side again that night, lying on a mattress next to her bed. I thought about staying awake, even though I had done so the whole night before. But some strange intuition told me it was OK to sleep, despite knowing her time was growing short. She held on for the morning light. When I woke in bright daylight, she was barely drawing breath but still responded faintly by trying to speak as I held her. She died in my arms on that sunny May morning. Tiny as a wren. Slender as a silver birch twig. I felt her last breath in this world exhaled against my cheek. I wanted to lift her up and carry her to the seashore. Honoured by the wind and sun. To the point where worlds meet. Watched by birds and waves. Instead, I watched as her body was taken away from me in a black, zipped-up bag, in the back of an undertaker's vehicle. I would never again have the chance to keep my promise and take her back to Cornwall.

Chapter 18
Harvest Mice and Hoverflies

Not many weeks had passed since then and the heat of summer was fully upon us, with far more ferocity than usual. The season was locked into an extreme heatwave that showed no willingness to break. I walked with Monty, later in the day once the intensity was dissipating, down by the river near the small 'almost nowhere' bridge. Rushes still grew on the riverbank here, stretching green leaves and purple stems well above my head-height towards the sky. In even the slightest breeze, they whispered constantly, but now the air was without even the faintest movement.

The sun raged in a glowing red sky as it fell towards the horizon. An angry sentinel refusing to relinquish its hold, trying to swallow every vestige of oxygen from the air into its fiery breath. The horizon was a charcoal-grey silhouette behind a pall of russet dust hanging over the fields. The vegetation was crackling, crisp and withered by an abnormal dryness, utterly without relief.

I don't know what made me glance down on the track to the spot where I was about to tread, but there at my feet were three tiny harvest mice, dead on the pathway, expired in the heat from thirst. Silky and golden, the largest no more than around five centimetres long and the littlest one, a baby, barely half its size.

A little wild family who had died together, each lying no more than its own body's length away from its companions and all facing each other. In life they would have been unnoticed. So small, in such a big field. Somewhere in it, they had had a home. A spherical ball of tightly woven grass, lined with silken fluff and suspended between corn stalks. Desperation must have driven them from cover, onto the hard path, sending them travelling in search of any form of moisture before they expired on the track. They would have needed so little. Mere droplets of water could have saved them all.

In all my life I had never seen harvest mice because they are so rare. These diminutive, furry creatures are so shy they would never normally have risked venturing from the cover of vegetation onto the path. I wept for their small lost lives. I wept for the world that was too busy with itself to notice. Helplessly I stood looking at them, wishing them back to life but knowing they would not move.

Minutes passed. As carefully as possible I lifted their minute, fragile bodies into the palm of my hand, cradling them together and marvelling at their golden satin softness. I had always wanted to see harvest mice in the wild. Why did they have to be dead? I plucked some large sorrel leaves from the field-edge and placed the tiny bodies onto one, all three together, all facing each other, as they were when I had found them. Then I wrapped a couple more leaves round them for protection and carried them to the riverside, laying them by the unnamed bridge in the Place.

Perhaps I was hoping that somehow by the water they would come to be renewed. I just wanted to give them water. The water that would have saved them and I couldn't give them while they were living.

Maybe I took them to the river because I could not take my mother to the sea. I wanted so much to save them. I wanted to save her but I could do neither. So, I carried them and left them there, on the riverbank, nestled among the leaves, where they would not be trodden on or disturbed. There was nothing more I could do. Nothing that would help either the mice, or my mother. I like to imagine that late in the evening, when day met night, by some magic of Place, these little golden creatures reawakened and went down to the river's edge for a drink of the water they could not reach by day.

The track was narrow, little more than a footfall wide in places. Thick corn on my left side, reeds on my right and the heat of late summer hanging in the golden afternoon, a verdant, brilliant counterpoint to the dull fog of loss. In a sudden rush, a storm of tiny hoverflies clouded the air around me, swirling upwards from the reed stems, filling the space with beating translucent wings and glowing bodies. Suddenly I was back in the dream-state, but a million times magnified. I've often seen large numbers of hoverflies on a hot day, but this was an insane amount. There must have been thousands. I found their incredible number comforting.

Once, one of these tiny messengers had been enough to tell me I was dreaming. Now I was surrounded by them. Almost inhaling them. Each one totemic. The same message repeated countless times and impossible to ignore: "You are dreaming! You are dreaming! This isn't real. Wake up! WAKE UP!"

At the sight of them I knew that if I could not say for certain how to define the boundaries of our waking world, then how could I claim to know who or what might be within it? Who is alive and who is dead if we are in a dream? What do those terms even mean? How can we be 'dead,' if what we think of as our life isn't real? Maybe I was dreaming. Maybe we dream this world into being. If it wasn't 'real' then I could change it, just like in a lucid dream. My dreams always used to be lucid. That clarity fades with the passage of time, whatever that is. But in every dream there always used to come a point where I would know that I was dreaming. From then I could direct the dream where I chose, moving through it as we do in the landscape of the physical world. *Why do I not still do that?* I wondered. Then my inner knowing told me almost immediately "You need to do it in the dream-state of your supposedly waking life! Then you will wake up."

It was time to move on. The fens were beautiful and would always be special for me but all my reasons for being here had gone. My biggest sadness was despite all the times I had promised my mother that we would move on together, I could no longer take her with me. I would never see her excitement at being told I had found us a new home, where we could go and be happy together. It didn't feel like there was any point in getting one now. Somehow nowhere would ever feel quite the same. It is the sorrow of the nomad, that those who die are left behind and the living know they may never return to the place of their loss.

At the retreat of the last Ice Age, reedy marshes formed in the place of the disappearing ice sheet. In these marginal spaces where the elements joined, there was nowhere to bury the dead. The land simply wasn't solid or permanent enough. You can't bury a body in estuarine marsh because the shifting ground means it won't stay buried. The people there may have used what nature provided and placed their dead onto rafts on the water, to be taken out to sea by the tide. It would have seemed both natural and magical. You go to the joining place of worlds, hand over the dead person to the elements, and they are pulled away by an invisible force towards the vanishing point of the horizon, like being able to watch the transition to another world.

Early in the morning when I was due to leave, I walked to the river again, knowing it was the last time I would go there. It was not unusual in the early mornings and late afternoons to find a few swans drifting along near the bridge. One or two, sometimes as many as four or five would pass. Elegant white beauties on the shining water. But this morning was different. First one appeared, gliding silently through the silver mist. Then another two. Then three more. Normally that would be all, but today they kept coming until a total of fourteen of them drifted into view under a shell-pink sky, through the ethereal mist.

Stunned by the sudden appearance of so many, I stood captivated on the riverbank. Might the diffuse sunlight somehow dissolve me with it as it evaporated and let me pass with it into some higher, larger state of being where nothing was ever lost? I could only wish. Monty touched my hand with his nose and the journey ahead beckoned us on. I had to go

Chapter 19
The Forest of Galloway

I headed north. I had to go somewhere. I couldn't stay with my friends forever and I needed my own place. Although the call of Cornwall was ever-present, I couldn't face going back there without my mother. I couldn't bring myself to go back to the places that had meaning for us and not share them with her. So, I went in the opposite direction. I drove to the west coast of Scotland, to visit friends for a while, whom I had not seen for several years. It felt like a relief to look around and explore somewhere new. At least that's what I told myself.

My explorations took me out on a soaking wet day. I left my friends' place in Darvel, driving southwards along the west coast towards the Forest of Galloway. I hadn't gone far before the rain progressively became so monsoon-like that visibility was at best terrible and all but non-existent at times. It would almost have been laughable if the situation wasn't so imminently dangerous. Torrents that completely defeated the wipers were sluicing across the windscreen like waves at sea, while I endeavoured to hold my car onto the angular bends that scraped themselves around the mountainside. Rocky precipice down to the rushing sea on my right hand, thickly forested cliff face on the left and a road that felt as though it might disappear off into the clouds at any moment.

It all added up to the surreal sensation that it was hard to tell whether I was driving a car on solid ground or might in fact be flying a small aircraft through thick cloud. It would have been disconcertingly easy to lose the ability to tell the difference, in one split-second, lethal error, and just drive off the side of the mountain. If I had, in that weather I doubted whether anyone would have noticed for a long time, maybe even days, and my friends were not expecting me home for several hours.

Stopping was impossible as there was absolutely nowhere to pull over safely. I was losing my sense of reality. In danger of literally losing my grip. At all times I was acutely aware of my young dog, sleeping peacefully in the back of the car, trusting me to protect him. "Dying here is not an option!" I told myself sternly. "You have to keep Monty safe. He's relying on you and he can't drive, so get on with it!"

With each passing second, I was forced to make the decision to live. The slightest lapse of concentration would have most likely proved fatal. The torrents of rain pelted me with irony. Mum had died in old age, at the end of her life. I was nowhere near the end of mine but could easily meet it very swiftly and prematurely here on this sodden road if I let my attention waver for even an instant. "Life is a choice!" said the drumming rain, "Life is a choice!"

But we can't choose to live when we are dying. For a moment doubt prodded at me. Then it was swept away like dead leaves clogging a stream and I focused into each instant. Somehow, in the flowing water surrounding me was the knowledge that even in the midst of dying we are alive. It is a step on the journey. Another road through a barrier like this cloud, beyond which the physical eyes do not see. Almost immediately came the deeper knowing, the wordless, resonant response, "We can choose to live while we are alive!" Water ran everywhere. The very fabric of the world seemed to be dissolving in it. Perhaps I was dissolving along with it.

I'm not sure how I managed it but amazingly I kept the car on the road, despite the fact that I couldn't see it most of the time. Eventually the invisible road turned itself slightly inland, becoming a forest road rather than a coastal road, which mildly relieved at least some of the danger. The tall trees provided a little shelter from the relentless rain, although thick cloud still swathed everything in grey blankets of fog and the tarmac was slick with flooding surface water.

The majestic trees would have been easier to appreciate if my shoulders had not been raised to my ears and my spine stiffened with tension from the horrendous driving conditions. I'm a confident, very capable driver and have clocked up many thousands of miles on the road, including in all sorts of adverse weather, which I usually tend to perversely enjoy. There are very few moments in my life where I can say I've been truly scared behind the wheel of a car or doubted whether I might make my destination, but this had definitely been one of them.

Eventually, I turned into a small side road marked for Kirroughtree Visitor Centre and followed it through a series of bends before emerging into a large, well-presented car park. The rain was beyond torrential, but nothing could detract from the immediate sensory impact of the wall of green that surrounded the perimeter of the parking area and soared skywards.

Emerald pines stood close and watchful, impenetrable to both eyes and ears, reaching for the lowering clouds. They filled the air with resinous scent and pressed shoulder to shoulder, on a slope that rose away steeply. Tall green spectators in a natural amphitheatre, they dwarfed the cars and pointed upwards, arrow-straight, to the clouds, rustling in the pelting rain as though in soft applause at my arrival.

This was not a welcoming place. It was not forbidding either; it simply didn't care whether I was there or not. It was ambivalent to whether I had made it through the deluge. It wouldn't have cared if I had died on the coast road with Monty. It didn't need us. Which was exactly how it should be, but still it lent no touch of comfort to the view.

I imagined the leafy applause held a faint note of sarcasm. The coliseum effect was emphasised by pathways leading off through narrow openings in the trees, like gates through a wall, in contrast to the flat, empty car park, lending the whole scene a gladiatorial feel. I half expected to be challenged at any moment by some wildly enraged combatant and the prospect of being required to fight for my freedom or my life seemed fitting. Excess adrenaline from my crazy drive through the clouds was still draining from my bloodstream and now I seemed to have stepped into some otherworldly arena.

The sense of exposure was even more compelling than the rain. But I still couldn't bring myself to take the closest shelter of the immediate forest edge. Something about the solidity of that green wall just repelled me. I didn't care if it offered the closest shelter. I turned across a swathe of grass on my right and headed for the further treeline, where I could see into it in stages.

The forest floor was a scented tapestry of long brown pine needles and fallen logs. Massive tree trunks formed bridges across the trails

and gave Monty a playground of challenges to practise hunting in. Gleefully he chased the scents of forest creatures, real and imaginary, round and round, paddling in the abundance of streams, jumping off gnarly logs and landing on the cushions of soft pine-needle leaf litter.

On small, furry paws, Monty hurled himself into the air as though he expected to fly. I felt lost, despondent and afraid. But because I loved Monty, I made time for him to have fun. He put up with all our car journeys because I always found places for him to play and experience life. In a forest where I would not otherwise have gone that day, I marvelled at its sheer living presence. We had walked into not just a collection of trees but also an entity. The forest was a living thing and the touch of its consciousness was palpable and strong.

We played there in the rain, among the trees and lush grass clearings, for a short while. I sensed that the forest was tolerating us but did not particularly like us. We did not belong there. I felt as though it put up with me, barely, because I had gone with a puppy and young animals were something it understood. It allowed us in to give him time and a safe place to play. But I would not have wanted to walk into the presence of that forest with an axe instead of a dog. Of all the things it told me, the clearest thing it said was that we should leave. Beautiful and impressive as it was, I was glad to do so. I wished it peace and drove away with Monty, in the rain, with a long road ahead of us.

Chapter 20
Red Kites

I couldn't face going back to Cornwall and I didn't know where else to go. There were lots of places I could go but I had no reason to be in any of them. I was placeless, separated from Cornwall by self-imposed walls of blame and confusion. I was lost without it and hadn't yet learned how to be free. My roots had been cut by the knife-edges of guilt and grief. The green lanes and coves felt inaccessible to me now. Mists had closed across the way back and I didn't know if any effort I made could part them again.

I told myself it didn't matter. I tried to convince myself that I would be fine if I went somewhere else. Somewhere new. I bought a house in a rush. In hindsight it was stupid but it was what I had become conditioned to thinking I had to do. I needed to leave my friends' place and I couldn't think clearly enough to find a better way. The unreal world was trying to pull me back in. I hadn't yet shed the expectations of the culture that surrounded me. But it gave me some time and a place of my own in which *Conversations with my Dog*, came together. It wasn't home, but it was a respite.

I set about completing the illustrations for it with growing determination. As I did, I started learning more about myself and what I wanted. As ever, Monty was my lifeline. The notes and drawings I had made of him had already become a fully formed book, ready to submit for publication. Except I'd never published a book before and hadn't a clue how to go about it.

I made a few tentative enquiries, when I could battle my way out of the choking fog of fears about things like how to make a living.

There were choices to be made. I could send the manuscript to one publishing company after another in the hope that someone not only liked it but that it arrived in the right moment in their schedules and budgets. That's the old way and great if it works. But failure can be as much down to timing as quality of work. Or try self-publishing. That would mean committing money to hope, based upon what I believed to be the value of my own ideas, while acknowledging that maybe no one else would like them.

Yet it felt right. I stopped talking myself out of it and called a few self-publishing companies to learn about the process. I didn't know one company from another, or how to tell good from bad. The first one I tried was informative but seemed very pushy and proceeded to send me emails every day. Then I got lucky. I called another company and said, "Help! I'm an artist and I've written a book! I'm pretty sure I can illustrate it too. I'd like to publish but I haven't a clue how! Can you tell me what I need to know to get the illustrations right so I don't have to do them twice?"

"Of course!" The man on the end of the phone laughed, pleasantly. "You know, mostly people don't ask those questions. They just do something and present it to us." We got on straight away. Whatever question I asked him, he gave me well-reasoned answers which were informative and helpful, not just a sales pitch. He told me he would summarise everything on an email for me so that I could read through it and then, amazingly, he didn't try to sign me up, he told me to go and think about it for a day or two and consider what I wanted to do.

I went off and did battle with the ghosts of old scepticisms. Artist? Author? Illustrator? Could I really be these things and dare to want to be successful enough to have a nice home too? The echo of my mother's words, which she had said to me before she died and so many times as I was growing up: "You don't know what you can do until you try!"

Over and again, it became clearer to me that I needed breathing space, in a culture that seemed determined not to allow me to have it; demanding, "Fit in, keep up! Do what everyone else does!" *Watch my life go by while I waste it doing things that aren't real!* Breathing space seems such an obvious wish but it is an increasingly rare commodity. I needed space to work out what was of value and what wasn't. To be sure of what was real.

Since Monty clearly knew better about these things than me, I relaxed and let him take the lead. If he told me that it was time to go out then we went, and every time I listened to him, I saw something or learned something which made things clearer. Whenever I aligned to my dog, he reconnected me to the wild and life became more straightforward.

The small burn at the bottom of the village ran swift and clear through granite stones, rushing and chattering. We followed its path, over the road out of the village and into the opposite fields, climbing a hillside of brilliant green. Overhead, Red Kite flicked russet wings against the turquoise blue and twisted elegantly on the breeze. Balletically poised above the green slope, uplifted on nothing but the clear air. Dancer on the wind, I could feel the piercing strength of her golden gaze upon me. Raising my arms to acknowledge her, I spun on the ground, moving up the hill. She spun with me and followed the line of my movement, dipping her flame-like wing-tips. Her mate came to join her as we approached the crest of the rising land. I opened my lifted hands towards them and stepped back to watch their dance.

Curving long tail points drew a calligraphy of fiery feathers against the sunlit sky. "Are you kites or phoenixes, beautiful birds?" I asked them. They twisted in answer into a spiralling near-embrace, turning towards the sky in a rush of flame-coloured grace. "What do you want me to know?" I asked them. "Make beautiful things," they told me. "And if the wind of freedom blows for you, dance with it!"

I watched them hunting together, while Monty played, chasing scents through the grass and running happily in the honeyed autumn sunshine. The kites hung suspended on the breeze. They called to each other as Monty hunted beneath them, watching the ground with golden eyes for mice disturbed by his activity.

At the summit of the hill, as Monty stood, naturally confident, silhouetted against the clear blue sky, the majestic kites peeled off, matching the line of the land. Agile aerial hunters, they flaunted their feathered athleticism, flirting in approval of each other's prowess. "Remember…" they said, "you don't have to fly alone to fly free!"

As soon as I went indoors, I called the publisher and agreed to send them the manuscript. From that moment, I started a learning journey from which I would soon not want to turn back. Being an artist is one thing; you can paint what you like. You make a painting and people either like it or they don't. But illustrating a book has technical complexities I had not needed to consider before. I learned on the job, grateful for the publishing team's patience with my questions and inexperience. I knew I had found the right company when, every time I asked a question, they answered it with clear and thorough explanations which exceeded my expectations. My time here was turning out to be extending my skills. I was learning to be more than I had thought I could before. Despite not being able to see many steps ahead, it felt like being on the right path.

I went into Castle Douglas to pick up shopping. The view from the road was a panorama of streaming sunlight and showers. Silver trails of rain hung from the clouds, following the path of the wind in curtains. Pale gold sunlight poured down through the gaps between statuesque, slate-grey clouds until it became hard to tell which was light and which was water. The whole scene was fluid. Dove-grey mists veiled distant hills in softness. "This is real!" called the wind.

I took Monty to the beach at Sandyhills. He raced along the soft sand, ears flapping and sparkling surf splashing from his paws, running in the fresh breeze for the joy of living. The Scottish coast was putting on a show of drama and beauty. Sunshine spilling in pools of brilliance onto the rising tide and dissolving the horizon into pure white fire. Emerald pines on the low, granite cliffs watched us playing. They were smaller than their counterparts in the Forest of Galloway. I'm not sure why but they seemed happier too, despite being buffeted by the sea winds, with nothing to separate them from the full might of the Atlantic but a tenuous strip of rippled sand. "This is real!" laughed

Monty, with eyes full of fun.

The sky always gives us warning of change. Driving back, I watched small clouds scurrying across the restless span. They raced in small groups, rushing for the curling blue hills, skirted by a smudge of dark pines. Where the road passed through a thicket of trees, a tracery of black branches spread starkly in front of the crystal light and spoke mysteries to the fading day. "This is real!" They rustled as we passed by.

Scotland was a beautiful land of wild, green forests and windswept beaches. I applaud the Scots for their common-sense approach in having a legally recognised right to roam, with no such thing as a trespass law. Yet even so, I had managed to be living in a village where the local farmer had bought up all the surrounding land and chained the gates shut to every field, despite a noticeable absence of livestock. He had put signs on the gates about cows, yet there were no cows, for miles in any direction.

I felt hemmed in. The only field available where dogs could be easily walked was a public one behind the local primary school. A designated patch of green. But within two days of arriving, I was chatting with a neighbour, who told me that the field had been sold and construction work was due to commence in a few months to build around forty houses on the field. My solicitor either hadn't picked it up on the searches or hadn't informed me. I would never have moved there if I had known. In that instant it was clear that I had made a bad mistake coming here and I would not be able to stay. The road loomed again and it was starting to look like a road to nowhere except an empty bank balance.

I longed to be able to walk, without restriction, without bumping into impenetrable barriers after more than a few feet in any direction. Here a wire fence, there a metal barrier caging a road…

I walked with Monty to Red Kite Hill. As soon as I approached it there was a strange stench of fuel and pine resin, mixed with a sort of metallic reek, hanging thickly in the air. As we emerged around the sweep of the hill, I saw that in a sickening confirmation of my decision to leave, the farmer had cut down the entire small wood, where the red kites had sat in the tall trees, watching the open green span. Only a hacked-up mess of stumps and splinters was left of the once tall pines. I suppose he got paid for them. The kites were nowhere to be seen. They were homeless now. They had vanished, like memories, into the blue.

That night, I dreamed that I was driving south through Cornwall to the Lizard again, along one of those roads where the hedges are so thick on each side it is like a long, green tunnel. Lys Ardh was still far ahead of us and the land had not yet opened out into the high moorland there which speaks of light and windswept skies. But I was heading the right way and I could feel it. I could see the clear space at the end of the tunnel of trees. It seemed far off but I could see my way!

Suddenly an idea occurred and I looked at the barrier of tree trunks in the hedges that contained me. I realised that I could see bright sunlight through them and open green spaces beyond. Although they were solid and strong, rooted in the earth, they were also flexible enough to be parted with my hands. I grasped two and pulled them apart enough to make a space I could squeeze through.

I let Monty jump through the gap and followed him into fresh, green Cornish fields. The dream felt hopeful and I awoke feeling invigorated. "OK, Subconscious!" I addressed my remaining mind, aloud. "Nice pun about the light at the end of the tunnel! Apart from that, what are you telling me with this dream? What's the meaning of going sideways through the hedge?"

"You are on the right road again!" it communicated instantly. "Think laterally! Your destination may seem far, but you're heading the right way now. If you look around yourself a little more closely, you might find you don't need to go all the way to the end of that long tunnel. Cornwall might be closer than you think. Your way out is close. All around you! Use your hands! Make your way out with your hands."

Think laterally! The command stuck in my mind. As did the message about my hands. Do what you love and it will lead the way home. Cornwall was calling. I stood in the dismal, wet field, where

the builders would be arriving soon with their concrete and bricks, and heard the sounding of a distant sea reverberating from that place deep within.

This always happens. Wherever I go, eventually it calls me back. It echoes from some place inside me that I can't put a name to, somewhere beyond sound or distance, and it will not let go. These are the moments when Mum and I used to just get in the car and go. When we couldn't help it any longer. In the middle of some random conversation one of us would mention Cornwall and we would just look at each other and ask, "Shall we go?"

Now she had gone on a different journey, without me, and though the idea of going back to Cornwall had not seemed the same since she passed, eventually, I knew I would return. Swallows migrate across oceans and deserts, salmon swim back upstream to the place where they were spawned. They do not stop to question whether they should or ask if they should maybe go somewhere else for a change because some of their number have fallen along the way. They return to the places which are right for them, those which they know by their inner compass. Where else would they go? My inner compass was pointing me firmly south back to Cornwall once more.

Chapter 21
Moving On

This time I had not the faintest hesitation in recognising that I needed to move on. This location was wrong for me. I had come to realise that when your inner nomad knows that a place is wrong, it will waste no time in urging you to leave. To ignore it is perilous, for the inner nomad draws upon the imprinted wisdom of many thousands of years of travellers.

I felt ill from being unable to resolve the mess my life was in. I wanted a home of my own, but I couldn't bear the thought of tying myself back into a job I didn't care for just to repay a debt. It felt like slavery. Working is fine when it is to make things we need, make a living and contribute to a community, but why should we be tied to huge debts, just to have homes of our own? It isn't natural. Debt is unnatural. The concept of owing money which isn't even real, because it is no longer anything solid, to pay for a real home just felt bizarre. Like buying reality with fantasy.

We should be free to make our own homes and lives, wherever we best fit in. These kinds of debts, despite being socially acceptable, are just a form of enslavement. Working all day doing something I didn't care about, while Monty got distressed at a dog minder without me, wondering where I had gone, just wasn't viable.

Writing was the path I hadn't expected to find. I wanted a home, with security and normality, but the red kites were dancing with my soul. I was rewilding, renewing myself and I could not turn back. My wild self was turning me into something else. Someone I had always been.

By the time the first book was published I had the manuscripts for two children's books completed ready to illustrate and the notes on ideas for several more. Uncurling and stretching inside me, like a bear waking from sleep, was a kind of growing self-knowledge. Was it a new place we were searching for? Or something else? Lifestyle, culture and society had dictated for too long what I must have, in order to live comfortably and reasonably. But what I really wanted was creativity, simplicity, learning, to live being comfortable with myself.

Maybe I could have these things and a place to live somewhere I had not yet been. But one thing that was clear was that it wasn't here. I had to get away. How could it be that in Scotland with its abundance of wild space I had chosen somewhere to live that had so little immediate access to any of it?

In retrospect it had been a move of great frustration and expense I could have saved but it had been a way of putting some pieces of the jigsaw into place.

I was putting myself back together and it had taught me what was important. I loved being an author and illustrating my books. The wild was expanding through my consciousness the way a river spreads when it reaches the sea. Monty was the reason for my first book, but there was so much more I could do. He embodied the joy of living and it was easy to find inspiration everywhere I turned just by observing his happy character. I loved drawing him. It didn't matter to him if I had gone in the wrong direction as long as I kept him safe. I re-prioritised my values because of him.

The next few months became an exercise in mental flexibility. One thing I noticed; when you change the questions that you are asking yourself you start to get different answers. Then you can change your life if you want to. Why was I still searching? Still on the road? I began to question whether the reason why I could not find a place I wanted to live in was because if I couldn't afford what I wanted then I didn't really want to. Only then did all this upheaval begin to make sense. It was time to do things differently. The time spent completing the illustrations was well worth it. The meticulous process of integrating images with words not only prompted new ways of thinking but left my remaining mind free. Re-alignment started to grow from the inner spaces. Seedlings of promise, rising to the light of new ideas. Those wild whisperings, which had begun with a conversation with an oak tree at midwinter, were becoming an integral part of my life. The way they had once been.

The more I worked, the more ideas I had and the more I learned about how to develop them. I knew I needed the freedom and capital to turn them into reality. Not to go back to just squeezing it in when I could find the time, around all the obligations that weren't mine. We can't escape ourselves. I was always going to do this. I just forgot for a while.

I suddenly recalled the 'books' I used to make when I was very young. I used to draw and write on sheets of paper, folding one page inside the other. Scribbled colours and magical ideas spread joyfully from one to the next. So why should I worry about not succeeding? If I set out to make books from a time before I even knew what publishing was, then I could hardly be surprised I was still doing it. The adage 'How would you live if you knew you could not fail?' stuck in my mind. It might be a cliché but it was a reassuring one.

We can't shield ourselves from what is within us. Parts of our brains are attuned to hunt. We may no longer live hunter-gatherer lifestyles but we cannot just remove that part of ourselves. Our instincts evolved to keep us not just alive but healthy from interacting with the natural world. The wind, land and sea speak to us in ways which are older than computers and the internet. Shelter, water, food. This basic triangle of life has kept us alive for millennia. The internet doesn't feature in it.

The year's circle was coming full turn since the beginning of my long journey with Monty, when we first set out from the Fens. Midwinter was quickly approaching again. The mess of the past year was drawing to a close and it felt like I had covered a lot of ground, but my heart knew there was still much further to go. I seemed to have traded one mess for another.

The interminable search for a house had come to an end but only because I ended it too quickly in a location I didn't like. I hadn't been brave enough to accept myself as the nomad. So, I had a home that wasn't home. I hadn't stopped searching because I hadn't found what I wanted. I hadn't had the courage to wait in somewhere else temporary while I learned what was most important. Temporary, temporary! I was sick of temporary! More than anything I wanted to start life again in a deeper sense than just moving house, but where? How?

The message of Red Kite danced in my thoughts. 'When the wind of freedom blows, dance with it!' The wild would come. I knew now that it never truly leaves us. "The wild will come." So said the sea that resonated from within. So said the wind passing by on the hillside and the rain on my face. It would come because I would welcome it, arriving to find us in a better place. Somewhere with room to move. No longer just seeping in from the margins, 'wild' would be central to our lives. The pillar that I based life around, not a pretty nicety for a corner of the garden.

I wasn't going back. A day would come, like the dawn of a spring morning. The thought that it might be possible to live differently was a hope I could no longer relinquish. A year after my escape, the artificial world was still trying to pull me back in, as if my freedom had angered it.

I would honour the wild by writing all that had happened in the year and more. Uncertainty loomed again but this midwinter brought with it the opportunity to see it as an invitation to create new life and adventures. This felt vital. The beginning of a new path. Nothing is more essential. Whoever we are, whatever our lives have been, we can always start a new path. We make the path.

I let the winter blow over us while I concentrated on the basics. We had the triangle of life and we had each other. We had the two fundamental extras of fire and a defensible position, which lift life from the level of immediate survival to comfort. Everything else would have to wait for us for a change. I wasn't going to chase; I was going to centre myself and pay attention to what I was calling to me.

"Stop!" I ordered myself. "Just stop running around in circles worrying about priorities which aren't yours." The learnings from my old karate lessons came back to me in new ways. "Don't weaken yourself by overreaching! That is how an opponent draws you off centre," I could hear my instructor telling me. "There is a circle around you at the extent of your reach. You deal with that! What is within your circle? If something is outside the circle that may be a threat, you wait until it enters but don't chase it. While it is outside your circle it doesn't matter." In the winter gales I took a long, hard look at what I had been drawing to my circle.

Spring was not far away. Even in winter I could feel it approaching, just around the corner. A prescient light, faint as the touch of dawn, was already pervading the new season. The year was turning. Winter loosening its grip even while appearing to still be locking the world in ice.

Monty's first birthday had passed in an interminable period of wet weeks. It felt like I was living inside a washing machine that someone had forgotten to turn off. Revolving in a permanent spin cycle of wet coats, soaked boots and dog towels. We went to Sandyhills beach and I watched him tearing up and down, splashing in the water, getting satisfyingly soaking wet. We were still wet but at least it was from having fun in the sea, for a change. My heart lifted to watch him playing in nature. Ecstatic silly grin and ears flying in the breeze like pennants streaming behind him.

He would tear around like this, happy just to run and play with me until I took him back to the car, sopping wet, tired out and covered in sand. His uninhibited playfulness was a contrast to my stress. I felt stuck. Not trapped like before, just lost and afraid. I longed to be on the road again with Monty. I was fed up with others telling me how to live. I had bought a house because I thought I had to. I needed somewhere to be but it wasn't what I wanted. I was stuck between worlds. The one I couldn't quite make and the one I kept being pulled back into. I craved the safety of simplicity, of things being uncomplicated. The simplicity of the wild was no longer a wish, it was a necessity.

I could hesitate no longer. Nervously, I put the house on the market. I started to make some enquiries with a friend who had a cottage I could maybe rent in the Lake District for a short while. Always a short while. Temporary again, but still a step forward and a step I needed to take. A step on the road south and maybe, just maybe I could find a way to part the thickets of my inner limitations with my own hands. Monty and I still had a long way to go.

PART 5
South

"Hmm, South it is then! I always like going South. Somehow it feels like going downhill."

Treebeard in *The Lord of The Rings,* JRR Tolkien

Chapter 22
Threlkeld

I have never been comfortable in locations which are surrounded by mountains or even large hills. I admire their beauty and can love the landscape there, but somehow, I always feel the presence of high ground around and above me, no matter how beautiful, to be a cause of uneasiness.

No specific event has ever caused it, it's just there. A strange claustrophobia. A counterpoint to my instinctive attraction to the sea. I can happily go underground into caves to explore and, if necessary, I can get into a physically confined space such as a tunnel without ill-effect. But if I travel into a mountain range, while I can appreciate it and respect it, I have a deep, instinctive need to leave as soon as possible. It is a sort of geographical impetus to escape that is somehow imprinted in me. Mountains trigger in me a compelling urgency to get over or through them. The feeling increases the longer I stay and doesn't lift until I can see the way out.

Yet Threlkeld was different. I wasn't sure what to expect. Somehow on my wanderings around the UK, the Lake District was somewhere I had missed before. The sense of confinement I had felt in Scotland started lifting as soon as I arrived there.

As December turned to January again, one full year's turn after I first planned to leave my house in the Fens, with Monty and with the passing of midwinter, the daylight was already starting to lengthen once more. It wasn't enough yet to really make things lighter, just somewhat less dark. Which was appropriate to my feelings.

My stay in Scotland had been exactly what I had sought and for that I reminded myself to be grateful, not frustrated. But it had proved to me that what I had been seeking was neither what I truly wanted nor what made me happy. It was true I wanted my own home and was glad to have one, but uncomfortably I had to admit there were things I wanted more. In that knowledge, things felt, just like the seasons, not exactly brighter but at least a bit less dark.

Perhaps if I had been able to afford what I wanted, somewhere in a rural location, with a garden for Monty, space to grow vegetables and walks on the doorstep then I would have been more than happy to stay put anywhere if it had left me with enough funds left over to finance developing my work. But if I couldn't achieve both then I was going to have to prioritise. It was becoming starkly evident that a house in a location which made me unhappy, with no access to wild spaces and no means to bring the ideas I was full of to fruition, would become a trap, not a home. Ironically, I could have found places such as I wanted further afield, but for some reason I just didn't see them. All I knew was what mattered to me had changed. I had to get back to something more real and until I could do that, I couldn't see the way ahead.

Time to leave again! I told myself that one day I would find a place for me and Monty, where we would be able to stay. But it wasn't here. No amount of delaying, wishing things were different would ever make it something it wasn't. The longer I spent dithering, the more it would just compound the problem.

Twilight was starting to come slightly later now. Tentatively, incrementally the daylight was extending and hinting of better times ahead, somewhere. As I headed away from the village, a burst of torrential rain and hailstones broke overhead, tossed dramatically at my windscreen as though some angry weather god resented my intended departure and hurled the entire contents of the sky at my car.

I drove through a deluge on the twining grey ribbon of the A75 as it slithered its way out from under the clouds. As I passed the Solway, heading south on the M6, the landscape on my right side opened up like a window onto the coast. Pale golden sunlight dissolved the scene into fluid brilliance, the expanse of water suddenly materialising, shimmering, from behind the mist. A short distance further, the imposing contours of the fells escaped the clutching clouds. The January sun poured a blaze of light across their profile, laughing at the weakening hold of winter. Luminous, beyond the rain spray and tinged with pale fire they seemed to float, surreal and beckoning.

Leaving the motorway and heading into the terrain that was starting to rise around me, my usual feelings of claustrophobia this would normally bring were notably absent. The shapes of the fell-sides, carved millennia ago by rivers of ice, were enchanting. Mostly green-clad, occasionally one would rise, pure white, frosted and gleaming, reflecting the winter sunlight through drifting mist.

The whole land was taking on a mystical air. It would not have surprised me if a unicorn had trotted elegantly into view across the fields, vanishing onto the snowy slopes in a sunlit, silvery twinkle. Unfortunately it didn't, but still I had to remind myself to concentrate on the road rather than stare at the landscape, hoping for unicorns, while driving.

A few quick turns through side roads brought me swiftly to the village of Threlkeld Quarry and a white stone cottage, on the end of a small terrace. It had a welcoming air about it, both from the outside and as soon as I stepped indoors.

Descending cloud was wrapping grey scarves around the ridges, speaking softly of impending rain. The mountain of Blencathra rose dramatically, skirted in emerald woodland, studded at its feet with house lights like a woman who, defiantly taunting winter, had gone out wearing a practical full-length green tweed overcoat, with diamond slippers twinkling underneath. It was the right place, for me at that moment in time. Inexplicably, strangely so.

This tiny village rested in a deeply curved valley, surrounded by peaks, yet I did not find them confining. Where I would usually have felt oppressed and even trapped by such an encircling ring of rock, here, rather than constrained, I felt as though some giant elemental being of earth had raised me up in huge, cupped hands towards the feet of the sky. Here, I was not confined but uplifted.

Along one side, the ridged contours of Blencathra mountain formed gnarly stone knuckles that pointed towards the house. Behind, the long, jointed curves of Saddleback resembled a thumb and forefinger pointing along the valley, curling down and supporting the village as the curious giant lifted it, childlike to the sky. A toddler showing a shining pebble discovered on the beach. Talisman raised towards the zenith.

It was completely and beautifully different from anything I would have deliberately set out to look for, yet exactly what I needed. I looked at the hillsides soaring up to frame the sky in slate and pearl and knew that here I could write. Here, I could breathe and do what I needed to for a while. I felt my awareness start to stretch and grow. I walked with Monty where the rain sparkled across verdant ground, thick with brilliant moss. We wandered where ice crystals danced around knobbly rocks and hung in the early morning mist that swathed the valley.

Despite the dramatic solidity of the huge, curving hills, they had a sort of semi-translucent quality that I had only experienced previously by the coast where the reflected light is so intensified that it seems to melt everything in its path. This place too was a meeting point, just different from those I had been used to. Here, the land did not tamely sit beneath the sky, but rose up in greeting to it, summits merging with low cloud and running with water. Crystal white and feather-soft greyness melting into the golden touch of sunlight.

The elements flowed through this land in equal measures. Earth was noticeably powerful, not just something underfoot. Here I had no sense of being hemmed in by earth but felt myself to be sharing in a celebration of it. From inside the cottage, the view of the mountain was perfectly framed by the living- room window. It stood like a breathing thing, massive on the doorstep. I was transfixed by it. Breezes spoke day and night, telling the stories of birds and their journeys among the clouds. Light danced through the clear air in the valley, patterning the hillsides. The sunrise was a vibrantly burning display of orange fire.

In the days to come, I would be mesmerised by the constantly shifting light. It had a fluid quality which blended with the crystal water that flowed everywhere I looked. It scattered rainbows, cascading from the broad shoulders of the hills, swiftly hurrying downward through fields and streets alike. On a rainy day the village roads had a permanent covering of clear, flowing water across their surface. It was like walking through a stream. Or a dream.

Here I rested for a while in this land of rain and sun, where water and light poured as one over the land. I knew that this place was beautiful, wild and elemental, but it was not home.

Chapter 23
Dragons

Long ago, people learned ways to represent their view of the world visually in drawings that could pass on information to others. The earliest maps were symbolic descriptions more than actual records of terrain. They tended to be pictorial representations of semi-known locations, surrounded by unexplored regions of which they could offer no description because nothing was known about what existed there. Here, the cartographers would write "Here be dragons!"

That dramatic statement may have been intended as a warning to anyone foolhardy enough to consider stepping 'off the map' into unknown territories, but it was also an enticement. For those who were willing to wander on unmapped ways and risk encountering fire-breathing beasts, the opportunities for discovery abounded. In these uncharted places the imagination could flourish, calling upon explorers to set foot upon new lands in the places where dragons lived.

Dragons! Mythical symbols of great power and energy. Inhabiting the unknown. Thriving in the wild, outside the margins of our narrowing perceptions.

It was easy to imagine dragons dwelling in these Lakeland hills. The very landscape seemed to be made for them. Or by them. Gullies in hillsides that could have been raked out by giant claws, scored the rock from crest to root. Magic poured through this place like rivers. Twisting streams tumbled through curving grooves which could have been carved by the long, coiling bodies of these giant creatures.

Wild beings and otherworldly ones lived alongside each other here as daily companions. Creatures both natural and supernatural co-existing comfortably where they have the space to do so. Suddenly, I dared to believe in dragons again and other things too. In a world where anything can exist, even the improbable can be true. In the part of my imagination that dared to suppose there were dragons, I wondered what else could be real.

I was off the map, in the margins, in search of the improbable. I had become a seeker of the mystical because every day it was starting to seem less unlikely. I was becoming a permanent resident of the margins, not a trespasser or one who had strayed in by accident. As my perception shifted, the margins expanded to become no longer narrow strips here and there but a fully-fledged domain in which almost anything might be possible. I understood now. Life is a creative project. Not just trying to find the way forward through a mess but choosing to sculpt something wonderful or write an inspiring story.

Old logic may have told me that it's easier to find your way if you have a map. But this was a more instinctive way than anything the conventions of Western culture understand. Newer or older? I could no longer tell. My previous mental maps would not serve me here, in these uncharted waters. With the decision to listen to the wild, I had outgrown them. Newer ideas were telling me, not to map. Not here. As soon as we map something, we define it.

"Don't map the wild," said the magic in the land. "It isn't supposed to be limited. If you do then it will stop being itself." *So, here I will not define. No cages of rigid outlines will I impose upon the untamed margins, enclosing the wild in a frame of words. Instead, I will show the door to bigger worlds and our wild hearts that touch them. I will take only the descriptions which the wild offers me, to place in front of others. I will let it show me what stories it wants to tell, asking for its voice, not assuming I know what it wants to say. Here, even upon these limited pages, may the wild be free. May it stretch and reach out, like the tendrils of fern roots or the branches of a tree.*

I wrote with Monty beside me and snow falling thickly outside. In a timeless moment, neither waking nor full sleep, I stood before a dragon in these hills. The dragon and I were facing each other and looking into each other's eyes and hearts. Dragons really do breathe fire, I discovered. Fire, the energy of transformation. It was Sky Dragon I faced and she offered me a choice. Flee, or accept the fire. I stood in the flame of the dragon's breath and was transformed.

Dragons abide in the rugged Lakeland hills. If one should chance to fly from the covers of this book and touch you, bid it welcome. Dragon fire has immense power and carries with it many gifts. If you do not flinch from its touch. Should you choose to stand, then know that once you have met a dragon, you cannot remain as you were. Dragon fire is a double-edged sword.

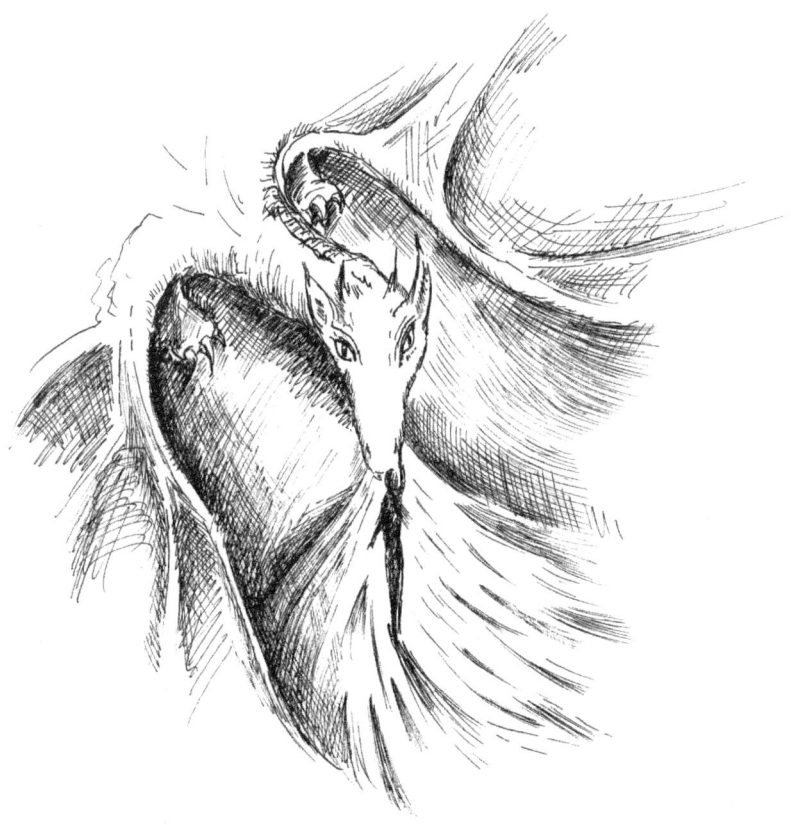

Chapter 24
Fire in the Hearth

It turned deeply cold soon after I arrived in Cumbria. A few days of pelting rain gave way to heavy snow, followed by picture-perfect blue skies, starry nights and frost. Winter froze the land in crisp ice. Wet, muddy earth quickly turned stone-hard and crunchy underfoot. The log burner in the cottage was a blessing, not just of warmth but also for embodying the simplicity I craved.

I was fed up with tariffs and contracts just to get warm. Fed up with being tied to other people's rules for the most basic fundamentals of survival. At one time it was this way; things were simpler. If the weather was cold, you lit a fire and it made you warm. The sheer simplicity of doing so again was liberating. I didn't want to have to worry about what agreement I was tied to. I didn't want any agreement at all. None except the daily contract of life between myself and nature.

The act of lighting the fire was a very basic pleasure. Some people might have found the need to do anything more than flick a switch inconvenient, but I found the ritual of laying the fire, kindling it, and ensuring it was burning steadily, to be relaxing and inspirational. A little slower maybe and surely there was a bit more challenge, but it was reassuring in its timeless simplicity. This honest act has been done by so many hands for thousands of years.

Our ancestors' eyes have gazed into the glowing embers for so long that somehow the action feels deeply imprinted on us. A stream of faces bridging the span of millennia have watched the flames of their hearths, mesmerised and warmed by dancing light. All their efforts and hopes embodied in those ritual motions.

They feel closer, those faces, when we raise fire in a hearth, as though somehow being drawn nearer to us watching the rekindling of flame and hope. By contrast the flicking of the switch has become disempowering. We no longer know or have any say in where our source of warmth comes from. If we flick it and nothing happens because there is some issue with supply, then many no longer know what to do or have the basic facilities to do it even if they did. Now, my mother had joined my grandmother and the two men I had loved, in that other-worldly place, just out of reach, and this winter, hope and light seemed even more important than before.

The dusty black grate came alive at the touch of fire. That moment of the first spark, igniting in a cold grate, raises hope and warmth. It is an invocation to the spirit of home. One which is somehow all the stronger for the physical action of having laid the fire yourself. It feels magical, the conjuring of light with your own hands. Set a fire in a hearth and you are personally creating an act to bring light and comfort to your home. It surrounds those you care about with cheer.

Despite being willing to leap unflinchingly into icy streams when out walking and paddle around contentedly in reed patches filled with the melted run-off from the frozen hills, engrossed in hunting some unseen quarry in the tussocks. Monty is very much a comfort-loving dog. He likes little better than to lie in front of a fire with his paws in the air, toasting his belly, snoozing and smiling.

The first time I sat down in front of the burner to light it, he looked on in curiosity to see what I was doing with these odd bits of wood in this strange thing that looked like a metal cabinet in the corner. But once he saw the first leap of golden flame and felt heat from it, he needed no convincing. Thereafter every time we went for an afternoon walk and arrived back just as the chill was starting to deepen towards night, he would head straight for the little hearth mat and sit on it, looking at me meaningfully, as if to say, "Light the fire!"

I usually had to work around him on my lap. To start with I pushed him away in case he got too close to the flames, but then I noticed that he never did. He wanted to sit as close to me as he possibly could and share the act of creating light. He had always had the same uncanny good sense around candles too. I took no chances, but the first time at ten weeks old, when he saw one lit on my coffee table, he stared at it with fascination. I had watched closely, preparing to either pull him away or blow out the candle as he inched nearer. Would he jump on it? Try to eat it or play with it? Stick his nose in it? No, he just approached it cautiously and slowly reached his nose forward until he decided that he was near enough and then stopped.

It was as though he had worked out quite naturally what it was, from being given the chance to do so. From that moment on, that was how he always behaved with candles or any naked flame. By his next winter he was perfectly familiar with fire, both in the form of candles and when I came to be lighting the wood burner; he immediately recognised that the creation of flame was something to be treated with respect.

Still, he loved the first touch of warmth, as light rose golden in the cold hearth. Happy as he was to run around in the snow, as soon as he got back inside, he knew to get his feet straight away off the cold flagstone floor to warm them up. So, if I stopped moving around even for an instant and sat down, I would quickly have Monty on my lap, using me for a foot-warmer. Which meant that lighting the fire had to be done whilst reaching carefully around an armful of spaniel. He never once leaned too close to the kindling as it caught fire, he just calmly waited for me to perform the task and in doing so he encapsulated the far-reaching relationship of human and dog, bridging the thousands of years of journeys for which these two have been together.

Warmth kindled. Fireglow shone in the depths of his eyes. Every time I looked into them, it felt like I was falling through time itself. Falling into the millennia-spanning conversation with all the years of shared understandings. So many hearths where fire has sustained hope and safety for human and dog side by side. So many long nights where each came to rely upon the skills and senses of the other. The touch of firelight on his fur spoke to me of all those shared moments, endlessly unfurling through the years. I rested my face against his neck, burying my nose in his fur and inhaled his natural, clean smell. In the long winter darkness, the nights were cold but they shone with stars and I was grateful, for the starlight and the love of my dog.

Chapter 25
Once Round 'The Wonky'

The snow had vanished from the windward side of the slopes and was thawing in patches, but the ground was still frozen hard. The streams were a haphazard game of chance. Some were standing locked in solid ice, waiting to be released, others had escaped and were chattering merrily about their freedom in a mad rush downhill, carving tiny rivulets through bright green turf and teasing their trapped companions.

The path onto the lower hillside required crossing a deep, free-running beck by means of a bridge that was no more than a thick plank of wood embedded in the bank and scrambling over a slightly lowered cutting in the dry-stone wall that offered access to the fields beyond and thereafter onto the fells. The first time I saw it, I wondered if Monty would cross it without slipping off. In fact, his paws barely touched the wood as he flew across.

From then on, he didn't bother with the plank bridge at all but would just leap the gap, gazelle-like, in a show of athletic flair. Incredibly, he could land with mountain goat-like precision, exactly on the narrow ledge of earth at the far side, without crashing into the stone wall or missing his footing. At a word of encouragement, he was onto the stone slab set as a crossing point into the wall, waiting politely for a second to check I could follow without landing in the stream, and was down the other side in a flash of lustrous black fur.

At the top of the field, just where it steepened and rose to meet the foot of the fell-side, was a fantastically twisted hawthorn tree. Gnarled black branches hung with pale lichens, each resting on the ground in a series of living arches. Entrances to some invisible building, perhaps. Thick roots curled and wove their way into the umber earth. It was the largest and undoubtedly the oldest hawthorn I have ever seen.

This was a Place and this magnificent, uncompromisingly wild and wonky tree was so intrinsically a part of it that it was impossible to discern where the tree ended and the Place began. Affectionately, I nicknamed it 'The Wonky.' Try as I might to find it a more auspicious name, something befitting its stature, stubbornly it stuck in my head as The Wonky and refused to be anything else. When the daily walks demanded by a strong, young dog needed to be squeezed into what narrow windows the weather permitted us, I learned that if I set out as soon as Monty would look at me with that "Let's go out and do something exciting!" sort of expression, then we could just barely make it up the hill, around The Wonky and back to the cottage before the weather closed on us. It took understanding, co-operation and a lack of hesitation to get the timing right.

"Come on then… Once round The Wonky!" I would tell Monty in response to his look and with no further invitation needed he would race to the door, fly across the stream and scamper gleefully off up the chilly green hillside. Going 'once around The Wonky' became more than just a brisk walk, it was a metaphor for seizing the moment and for trusting each other's instincts enough to just act and go, not stopping to over-think. Vibrant green moss, spongy and thick, cushioned every footstep. It grew everywhere, punctuated by forest-green reeds. Like a child's drawing, the whole scene seemed slightly too colourful, too naive to be true.

Monty, normally quite obliging when called, would have moments of going crazy snuffling in patches of long dark reeds. His interest in the few sheep that were dotted around was minimal at most. Unless they could fly or hide in a clump of long grass they seemed to hold little appeal for him. The possibility of finding something that might fly, even if it could be hiding behind the smallest clump of leaves, was a much more inviting prospect and he would determinedly set out to thoroughly search every single tussock, sometimes more than once.

Tiny buds on hawthorn, ash and hazel, far from breaking or even showing any signs of softness, were still present and swelling, eager for spring. Each one a talisman of new life. With every sight, every moment of noticing, the gap of separation between me and the wild was closing, little by little. With it, home was becoming not a place or a building but a way of being.

Snowdrops broke the icy ground with spears of bluey green leaves in sheltered corners. Almost immediately the first gorse flowers followed with a flourish of gold. Tiny catkins, still hard in their purplish cases but already swinging in the January breeze, taunted winter with a cheeky wave goodbye of their tiny fingers. Hawthorn twigs shone, gleaming bronze and promising fresh leaves to open on the spring air as soon as the sun warmed just a little more.

Chapter 26
Mum

I have often wondered what it was that bound us. There was something almost indefinable, which felt quite different to the obvious relationship or any shared interests. It was subtler than that. It has taken me until now to recognise that part of it was our shared love of the wild. Perhaps we were both children of the wild. You were my mother, but you were more than that, you were wild and transcendent of all familial connections. We shared our journey for a while. When our paths were dark you spoke of hope. We found our way through, coming eventually to the narrow trails across the Lizard cliffs, where we walked together enjoying the freely moving air. The sun and wind browned our skin and we talked of dreams and mysteries.

It was you who first taught me to put seeds in the ground and watch them grow, delighting in the tiny shoots and unfurling young leaves. Little viridian flags, each one a miracle. It was you who understood, when the baby blue-tit mistakenly flew into our kitchen and got stuck inside the window, why I wanted to be the one to pick it up and return it to freedom outside. "Wait!" you told my father when he tried to intervene. "She just wants to hold something wild in her hands." You let me take the youngster to freedom outside. You used to watch those feathered babies, nestled in the hedges, tucked into hiding places amid the foliage, gazing out with startled expressions and tufts of soft fluff sticking out in all directions.

You were the one who taught me to move quietly in nature, to do nothing hastily and then wild creatures would come to me if they wanted to. You showed me how to be someone who blended in with their environment and offered no challenge to wild things. To sit still if a bee landed on me and just wait until it flew off again. You waited while I climbed trees in the woods and laughed with me when I stood out in the pouring rain, getting soaking wet when the long summer heat broke into refreshing torrents that washed dust and sweat from hot skin, teaching me for the first time that rain is a blessing.

We were both just children, but somehow, along the way, I had forgotten that. I lost sight of your innocence in a world of duties and commitments which I came to believe were essential. Why do we surrender ourselves to the stress of worrying and give away our power? When we come back, I hope we are sisters. We will play and laugh together, dancing in the grass and staying out all day talking about amazing things. We will show each other shells and pebbles, pretending to bring gifts of treasures from far-off lands. We will sit on the bank of a stream, wiggling our toes in the water and swinging our feet together. We will be happy and fearless, climbing trees, watching birds and wild things in their secret lives.

Even if we do not remember this life, we will know that we have known each other before, because the sun on the water will tell us and the voice of the wild will whisper ancient knowledge in our ears. When we walk, I will take your hand in mine and we will be best friends for all our lives until we grow old together side by side once more. If our bodies become frail, our wisdom and love will just grow stronger with the passing days and outlast all dreams, as illusions fall away.

I will reclaim and re-sow the seeds of goodness you gave to me. I will tell of how we walked together in gardens and woodlands, on high moors, by the sea, and all the things you showed me. Skylarks above the cornfields, spinning upwards towards the endless blue. You were the first I stood watching them with. Soft-feathered owls with golden eyes. The rich hues of amethyst, lapis and amber. All the names of artist's pigments. How to cook good food from basic ingredients so I'd never go hungry even if I had little money. How to recognise every herb and spice by smell and how to know if food was fresh or going off without needing a label. How to recognise plants from as soon as

I was old enough to walk. The birds in the hedges and the seasons of the year.

You were a giver of knowledge, and the best of everything you had you gave me freely. You taught me the sounds of letters while I was still a baby, placing my fingers on your lips so that I could feel the sounds and copy them. As soon as I could hold a coloured crayon or a stub of pencil in my hand, you taught me how to write the symbols for those sounds and gave me my first alphabet. You offered me that leap of understanding that the sounds people made could be turned into marks on paper.

It was like magic! I fizzed with excitement from the roots of my hair to the tips of my toes. "I can't teach you everything," you told me, "But if you can read, you can always find out what you need to know." Because of you, I gained a love of reading so profound that I didn't stop with English but continued with any language which had a different alphabet, so I could feel that excitement again.

I learned to write stories, sitting at your kitchen table, the one with the shiny 1960s pale blue melamine coating that you never minded how much paint or crayon I got on it because it would just wipe clean. Is it right to share the gifts you gave me? I don't know. But I can give them new life this way. More life than just my own. You filled me with confidence to draw, write and create. Is it right to share the things you taught me? Or did you mean them to be just for me? I still don't know, but if I speak them I can breathe life into them.

Maybe your ideas will come to flourish in someone else's life. Maybe they will travel around the world and give energy to new stories. Perhaps someone will have new adventures somewhere with the confidence you gave them, even though you never met. Or maybe even someone who didn't have a mother like you, full of courage, love and hope, will be touched by your blessings because I shared them as much as I could. Maybe. I can't give other people all these things you gave me, but I can give them the inspiration to find them for themselves. If they do, there is a chance they too will pass on some of what is good in this world and protect it for all life's children.

You filled our small kitchen with smells of herbs, spices and the rich aromas of coffee, roast dinners and baking. You filled me with encouragement and the determination to stand up for myself. We might have been monetarily poor, but my childhood was rich with the scents of oil paints, turpentine and linseed oil. Your old biscuit tin full of twisted tubes of vivid colours was a treasure trove you shared freely. Each shade with a magic of its own. Once I'd progressed past the earliest stages of learning how to use brushes respectfully, you taught me how to use proper artists' pigments from the outset without stopping to give pause to those cheap, kiddies' boxes of hard watercolours that no one can learn to paint properly with.

I learned the vocabulary of burnt sienna, cadmium yellow, crimson alizarin, Prussian blue, titanium white, before I knew anything of technology. Apps didn't exist. The internet didn't exist. We didn't even have a landline phone. The signal for our black-and-white television relied upon Telstar, revolving in low-earth orbit, and went off at ten o'clock in the evening after the satellite passed out of range. The screen image contracting down to one little white square that seemed to shrink into the distance. After it vanished there was nothing but the snow of interference until morning.

Paints, words, colours and paper can protect us from the unreal world as we grow. They don't entirely block it, but they can shield us from it for long enough for the natural functions of our brains to develop fully, without being inhibited by apps and virtual realities. My early years were abundant with glowing colours and the joys of imagery shared. Flowers, trees, all the weathers and seasons, the wild world was speaking through us both and we were bound in love. Small wonder that my favourite subject matter was always the wild world; the landscapes and all the birds and animals living within them.

You showed me living things at every turn and taught me their names. You showed me blackbirds in the twilight, speckled thrushes in the sunshine and cheeky stub-tailed wrens in the bushes. We laughed at fluffy sparrows cheeping and fluttering and always we shared respect for living, growing things.

Not only the artist, but the navigator of life too. You taught me how to drive properly, looking as far as I could see down the road, not just to the next obstacle in front. As on the road, so too in life. This is the wisdom of the nomad. So many journeys we went on together, without ever really understanding how fast life changes. Until eventually we came to Cornwall and walked in the High Place on the windy paths through the flowers above the waves. Your eyes were the colour of the sea, multi-shaded and twinkling. Will I remember them when I am old? If I'm old.

We walked those uplifted paths among the thrift as you were growing old. You were coming to the end of the time we had together, although we didn't know. While there is any time left, we don't want to know it is leaving us. We'd rather imagine that we can stay the way we are. But if we could freeze time we'd never grow. We'd never learn beyond who we've become and we'd never find the next horizon. Now you have gone beyond that horizon and I can only hope one day we meet again on some wild, free path, somewhere on our souls' journey in the forever.

For a while, we forgot, as people do, that we are not the dramas of our daily lives and stresses. We forgot what mattered, distracted by things that we told ourselves were important and went off on diversions from our bigger journey. You came with me, bravely, hopefully, you followed where I led. You trusted me. You came along for the journey wherever the road took us. I wish I could forgive myself all the times I forgot that you were my fellow traveller. When we enter dark places, playing out the narratives of the people we think we are and shadowed by the ghosts of fears that grow from the unreal world, it is too easy to forget our bigger selves. I forgot the same wildness that moves in me flowed through you also. The same love.

And now, I am without you here. Or so it seems. So, I will hurl all my doubts and fears into the fire of hope that maybe things like love and life are stronger than both of us. *Fuck it! I am not going to sink in this tide of sleepy ignorance. I will not surrender to sadness and the illusion of loss. Fuck regret and guilt too! This is not real!*

The hoverflies showed me, we are dreaming. We dream this world. We are not the bodies or stories we come to believe ourselves to be. I don't care if there were things we got wrong. We were so much more than those. A world full of regrets for stupid mistakes I made will get me nowhere and still I will be stuck, bogged down in them, bound to them. What good are they? You made mistakes, I made mistakes. Love transcends them. We have a choice. Love is choosing the brighter path.

I went with Monty to the fell-side by The Wonky. When I can't make sense of something I always go to the wild. Maybe loss isn't supposed to make sense. Perhaps it is meant to be a doorway into mystery. The sunlight was dancing across the fell-side, but in my mind's eye I could see it in the High Place, burning a path of white brilliance across waves to the horizon.

"Teach me!" I yelled to the wild. I may feel pain and loss, I decided, but I will not allow them to make me dishonour all that love and learning with surrender! I will throw all that pain into the fire of the sunlight. Offered to the wild in a strange kind of hope. With a casual flourish of a silver wing, Sky Dragon emerged from behind a pine-fringed boulder outcrop, rising on the air. "I gave you a great gift!" she sighed in a tone of mild rebuke. "When are you going to learn to use it?"

"I don't understand."

"Yes, I've noticed!"

I sat on a flat stone, slightly curved and hollowed into the shape of an old, worn seat. Sky Dragon focused on me with clear-eyed regard and spoke with the voice of the wild. "If you had not loved your mother, you would not feel pain. Look behind the curtain of your grief and there you will find the love is still present. You mourn for the loss you think has happened but look within. What do you find?" I did as she instructed. Then stopped in shock.

"Within!" she urged, at my hesitation, as though hurling me off a precipice to see if I could fly. With the merest hint of a throaty roar, just a flicker and suddenly I was there again in the fire. "If you can crack open the shell of your own darkness and find the light inside, you will have discovered inner fire!" Sky Dragon lifted effortlessly into the air. "Use what I gave you!" she reminds me. "And remember... all dragons are shapeshifters. Sometimes when you see me, I may appear as another creature!" Then she was gone.

As she departed, I let her gift settle into experience. Inside us is light. Behind the clouds and colours of our emotions and thoughts. Burning light. To draw upon it will transmute pain to joy. "Use the gift!" I heard Sky Dragon call from somewhere far above and I understood. Perhaps if I stepped into the place where all is light, I could make real change, not just trade one illusion for another. I could not bring my mother back but maybe, in the light of that fire, even now, I could return our relationship to one of innocence and let us be children again.

We Are Children

Life is fleeting. Life is rare.
You were such a gift.
Are you still there?
Are you in the High Place,
Watching the sea?
Did you find your way home?
Or do you wander, like me?

We are children. We are wild.
We are travellers,
Under the skies.
Our hearts are nomads,
Our spirits free,
For we are just children,
On the shores of the sea.

Part 6

Returning

"Our deepest fear is not that we are inadequate. Our deepest fear is that we are powerful beyond measure. It is our light, not our darkness that most frightens us.

It's not just in some of us; it's in everyone. As we let our own light shine, we unconsciously give other people permission to do the same. As we're liberated from our own fear, our presence automatically liberates others."

A Return to Love, Marianne Williamson

Chapter 27
Midsummer Promise

I had a promise to keep and I was going to keep it come what may. It was the promise which after all my wanderings would take me back to that southernmost tip of Cornwall. To the High Place, full of light.

I went back to scatter Mum's ashes in the spot she had asked me to, as I had assured her that I would when she was dying. It gave me the reason to return. To tell myself that I was allowed to go back there. Just after dawn on Midsummer Day as the light was rising to its peak. It was a Place which had been special to us, where we had laughed and been inspired together, by the sea and the sky. Where we had been carefree, or at least as close to it as I'd ever known us be.

I didn't ask anyone. There are some things that should not require permission. Scattering the ashes of a loved one, in an open place, affecting no one and seen by no one, is one of them. I had no intention of making it a request to anybody. There was no way that I was going to do anything other than keep my word to her that I would perform this action where she asked me to.

Finally, I found my way back there with Monty at my side. There was a sense of inevitability in returning and as I drove the familiar road, I found myself wondering how I could have ever thought of doing anything else but returning here. It seemed stupid to think of leaving. I retraced our steps down the long, serpentine lane out to the coast path, as first light started to turn the sky rose-pink.

My feet would have known their way even in my sleep, I've walked that way so many times. The merging of dream and waking states flooded over me again, washing me into the landscape. When I reach this point, I always feel as though I have been through a series of half-visible doorways. The last of them is at the end of the deep, walled lane where it emerges through a gate onto the trail through the short grass above the cliff path.

In the springtime the dry-stone walls are smothered in countless flowers. A rainbow of pink, mauve, yellow, white and blue. For years, on the far side of the gate, next to the field edge, had stood a wooden post as high as a telegraph pole. It was linked to nothing and served no apparent technological purpose even if it had once done so. But it added something to the mystery of the place. A kind of punctuation mark to the southernmost end of the lane, after which the world opened to the wild again.

Puzzled, Mum and I jokingly referred to it as 'The Lamp Post' because it reminded us of that very same object in C.S. Lewis's wonderful *The Lion, the Witch and the Wardrobe*. That lamp post had stood, in the middle of a wood, discovered by children as they entered the magical land of Narnia through the back of a wardrobe. This one seemed equally out of place in its surroundings and yet somehow was also perfectly a part of them. It belonged, yet it didn't. But like its counterpart, it too marked the entrance to a magical world. A doorway to high cliffs, watched over by ancient stones, serenaded by skylarks above a turquoise sea, beyond which anything might be possible.

As I walked the serpentine lane, the ashes were strangely heavy. I was surprised how hard it was to carry them. It was almost as though the box I carried did not contain ash, but a black hole, infinitely small but heavy and pulling everything towards it. All matter, all light. It needed setting free. Free to take its place in the Universe. It needed releasing into a Place with enough magic and a strange kind of power that could cope with even a black hole. Somehow to transform it and not get pulled in.

It felt indeed like I was carrying the weight of a small galaxy around. For a year I had taken them everywhere in the car with me, through all the disruptions, just to keep them safe. I couldn't bring myself to put them in a box in storage somewhere, like a toaster or an old cushion. So, wherever I went on my journey they were wrapped up in a sea-coloured scarf in the boot. Now it was time to release them to the wild.

I was struck by how fine and light on the air the ashes were, silvery grey and soft as feathers. They were exactly the same shade as the rocks. The tiny fragments blended perfectly with stone and soil, dropping between the grasses and wildflowers, the finest dust just blowing away and dissipating on the breeze in softest silver clouds, vanishing from sight in seconds. She was becoming part of the landscape she loved. It felt good to see the starkness of death turn into something gentler and more natural in the open, sunlit air.

With each light breath of air, the black hole dissolved. I knew this was the right place to do this and she had told me to come here for a reason. We had marvelled at the light here many times, though not with this moment in mind. Here the light is strong enough to transmute even a black hole.

I felt subtly lighter, relieved to have kept my promise. I hoped she knew. The colour seemed to have come back to the world a little more. A light wind lifted the ashes into the clear air, handful by handful. It was like feeling the Universe breathing. It seemed to accept them as the silver dust merged with it, thinning out, getting fainter and fainter until I could no longer see them. Until eventually the very last handful was gone. I had nothing physical left now, but the faint trace of silver grey on my fingers. No more hugs for me. Just fresh air. No last chances for me to give her all the hugs I should have done but never found time for, no more sparkle in her eyes when she laughed at some joke we shared.

The larger particles had fallen onto the cliff face among the flowers and in the crevices of the rock. I told myself that the tiniest ones weren't gone, they were just being carried around the world and the biggest ones had fallen deep into the ancient rock that she loved, embedding themselves into it where nothing but the power of the wind and a great passage of time would ever remove them, if indeed it could.

I made myself promise to relish life, even if I didn't feel like it, to use this moment as she would have wanted me to and grab my life and wring every possible moment of enjoyment out of it. But that didn't stop my heart from breaking. Determination and promises felt like a cold substitute for her smile and the sound of her voice.

There was nothing to draw the attention of an unknowing passer-by to what had taken place there. No message of commemoration to say to a stranger, "My mother's ashes are here!" just a few tiny flecks of silvery dust on the red earth and grey rocks, blending perfectly with the surrounding land they were becoming part of. There was the natural significance of the Place, to mark them. More durable than any handmade sign. Perhaps this was the best possible tribute she could have.

I went back, along this path where we had walked many times together. Somehow, I had always thought we would do it again together. I wanted to see the spot again. It felt good to see the ash merging with the landscape there, as I knew she wanted, but still I wept inside, asking, "Is this all that is left of my mother? Ash? How can that be? My funny, curious, big-hearted mother. How can someone warm and wise be turned to this pale grey stuff?"

I couldn't shake off the idea that I had left her out there somehow. That her spirit would be out there on the cliff path when evening darkened the sky and the rains came. She was always the first to love the open skies and daylight, but also the first to love getting in when evening came, to a warm place, and putting the lights on. She would always make home cosy as night fell, closing the windows, drawing the curtains and putting something tasty on the table.

But I had kept my promise. I had brought her home. Now I needed to come home too. The realisation was inescapable. Nowhere else was home to me, or ever could be. There was no point moving to another part of the country just because it might seem easier, when I always just ended up longing for here and coming back. So, now all I had to do was achieve the impossible.

I am glad I got to spend her last days and moments with her. But it showed me what I don't want to happen when I eventually follow the same path. I don't want to die in an enclosed place, surrounded by medicine and well-meaning people in gloves and plastic aprons. People who know nothing of my life and force me back into the artificial world of form filling, disempowering rules and protocols to suit their convenience, just because I'm old. Numbing my senses with morphine, containing me indoors away from the wild, where it is 'safe.'

I don't want to breathe my last breath on air that's been through an air-conditioning unit, or worse yet, a ventilator, trusting to nothing more than hope that someone will be true enough to enact my wishes, but not sure. When that time comes, I only want the space to die on my terms, naturally, with my ashes to be scattered in the same place, open to the same sea breeze. At the feet of the ancient one who watches the waves as the Universe unfolds.

But who will care for me enough to see my ashes brought to the High Place? Who would be both determined and strong enough to make the journey to scatter them there? I have no answer for that. I have no daughter to leave behind, as I am left, to honour that last wish. She had me. I have no one. At least no one who is particularly likely to outlive me. It had taken scattering her ashes in this Place to show me what home is.

Chapter 28
Concrete and Serendipity

I had come with no hope of staying, just the intent to keep my promise. Nothing else. But this time something was subtly different. Something that was beyond definition. This time the place wouldn't let me leave.

I hadn't expected that. It started with an enormous slab of concrete that quite literally blocked my path. I hadn't been able to concentrate on booking somewhere to stay, once I knew that the old places were no longer available. So, I left it until the last minute. At short notice, I couldn't find somewhere at anything vaguely like a sensible price in Lizard village or nearby, so I booked somewhere closer towards Camborne and told myself that on Midsummer's Day I would just have to drive over to Lizard before sunrise.

The description online stated that the place I had chosen was down a long lane which was bumpy but that it would be suitable for normal cars. I left early in the morning to make sure I completed most of the journey before it got too hot. Roadworks and diversions around the construction of a new bypass added an extra hour and a half to my journey.

When I finally arrived, the long lane was indeed passable, in my perfectly average car. However, when I reached my destination and attempted to turn into the drive from the lane, I accidentally went next door first. The neighbour, a cheerful woman, pleasantly redirected me and before I left her driveway she offered, "You can park here if you want, to save you driving over that awful slab!" I casually waved her comment away, with thanks, replying, "It's OK. I'm sure I will be fine." I hadn't seen anything in the entrance to the correct house which looked as though it presented a problem.

I backed out through her gate and tried to go through the right one. With the most horrendous grating noise, I promptly ran the base of the car aground on a huge slab of concrete with squared edges, half buried in the ground between the gate posts. It didn't show up from the lane as it was in shade. Over time, with the passage of vehicles over it, the hard core and loose gravel alongside the slab had become pushed away by tyres, leaving the concrete edge protruding and a dip next to it.

Swearing vehemently, I pulled the car forwards again, with an equally horrible noise from the underside of the vehicle, turned in the friendly neighbour's drive and went up the lane to back into the drive from the other direction. It had to be possible, because vehicles were on the drive, so they must be able to leave. Not only did I run the car aground again, with an even worse noise than before, but it was now completely stuck on top of the slab, accompanied by the horrific sound of grating metal when I tried to manoeuvre in any direction.

The woman who was hosting me came out and suggested that I try a different angle. Her huge dog had also come to check things out and persisted in asserting his presence by barking loudly and constantly at the proceedings. Once I explained I had done so already and my car was now stuck beyond moving, she fetched her husband to push the car off the concrete obstacle. I was shaken and distressed. After a long journey the car was now hot and my concern was for Monty, in the back, who needed to get out and run around outside.

Weary and with frayed nerves, I knew with complete certainty that I did not want to stop here. It wasn't suitable for Monty with her dog and it was definitely impractical for my car. When I said as much, her comment was, "Oh well, your car is very low!" To which I replied that it was a perfectly ordinary Astra, not a fancy sports car or something with dropped suspension and her advert said the venue was accessible in a normal car.

Unbelievably, they looked surprised that I was upset. I felt like saying, "I came down here to scatter my mother's ashes, not to get my car ripped to tatters on some stupid piece of concrete that you haven't had the sense to make safe!" But speechlessness had overtaken me. I just couldn't gather my thoughts and get coherent words out. The woman suggested airily, "Well, you can park in the layby if you like. It's about a quarter-mile up the lane and you can come and go from there." My expression must have suggested otherwise because she added, "But, if you don't want to stay, we will refund you the booking, minus the cleaning fee." I said I would go and sit in the layby for a minute and think things over.

I sat in the layby shaking. I didn't have anywhere else booked and everywhere online had been busy or very expensive. I had no intention of staying here. Clearly the Universe was emphatically telling me not to, in the form of literally blocking my path with a giant piece of concrete! I could sense the spirit of my mother, as clearly as if she was sitting in the passenger seat, saying to me "For goodness' sakes listen!" I listened. I left.

I remembered the first time I had ever come to Cornwall with her. I had been telling her about it for a couple of years and saying we should go. Until one spring, I was living with her and we declared, "Let's go away." We didn't have a booking on that occasion either. We didn't know anywhere on the Lizard. Previously I had been a little further around the coast, to Coverack, with Robin and I wanted to go to back to that approximate area of Cornwall, but not to the exact same location. With a spontaneity which was uncharacteristic for her at the time, Mum suggested "Let's just pack some bags and go? Let's drive south as far as we can and find somewhere when we get there!"

That was how we had first come to Lizard village, to the High Place above the sea. "Have confidence!" I felt like she was urging me now, from the passenger seat. "Just trust yourself and go." So, I went. I drove away towards Lizard, knowing that it was where I was meant to be and if anywhere in the world could make things right, it was that High Place and its magic.

I asked a few of the usual places in the village if anyone had a room available for the week, but no one did. Unexpectedly though,

Caerthillian guest house, a friendly, Wedgwood-blue and white place in the village centre, had a room for the next few nights. I would have to leave by the 20th, the day before the summer solstice. But it would do for a few nights. The host was fine with Monty sharing my room, charged a reasonable rate and even offered to put the fresh produce I had bought for my stay at the cottage in their fridge.

Gratefully I accepted and before I had been there for a day, he offered me a phone number at breakfast and said, "Call her, she may be able to help. They are just in Ruan Minor up the road and have places to let." Curiosity piqued, because I had not seen anything at all available online in Ruan Minor, I phoned. My call was answered by a young woman who I liked as soon as she spoke.

That was how I found the farm. Magical place of ripening apples and secret shaded green corners. I would never have found it if I hadn't been told how. Through a small gap in the tall hedges which was almost invisible from the road, just like my dream, was a long, narrow lane that drew no attention to itself and meandered between bushes, vibrant with birds and wildflowers. It was a lane leading to sanctuary and inspiration.

Above the village and distanced from it by fields, resting below the crest of a slope, it tucked into the land on the seaward side, sheltered by trees. Like a bubble, this place existed in a time-frame entirely of its own. A secret within a secret. A spell within a spell. Beyond, the lane petered out into lush fields with faint tracks that wove their way towards the sea in the cheerfully haphazard manner which things always seem to have here.

The land began to unwind my thoughts. I could feel them dissolving with the sunlight and rain. Old patterns blew away one by one across the sea with the clouds. One walk at a time, I let myself open to the possibility of being what this land wanted me to be. I thought laterally. If I couldn't think straight, I no longer tried to. I allowed myself to think in circles instead, or curves, or whatever else seemed right. Nothing in this land is straight, so why should my thoughts be! The view of the sea from the highest fields was picture-book perfect.

A beckoning adventure of deep mysteries. I knew with the clarity of morning light that the Lys Ardh was somewhere I never wanted to leave. I knew it but felt helpless. What could I do, when the one place I wanted to live, where I *needed* to live, was somewhere I couldn't afford to be? "You kept your promise to me," Mum said. "Now you must keep your promise to yourself!"

This time, I hadn't come with the hope of finding somewhere to live. I had given up thinking that might be something I could have. I'd missed my chance. A sick fog of stress tried to claim my thoughts every time I realised that I could no longer afford to buy somewhere here. If I had done so straight away when I first came, perhaps I could have bought something unsuitable, maybe in a town, but I had hesitated. I had to look after Monty. My loyal best friend. I kicked myself repeatedly for the chances I had turned down. The clouds of doubt and self-recrimination surged.

But a fresh kind of hope was growing stronger by the day. In reality, I would have always gone back to the Fens for Mum and it would have always followed that I wouldn't know where to go after her death. So, why regret what was inevitable? It had taken a while for me to be able to say that I knew I belonged here, in Cornwall, but I couldn't leave. I could go and buy a small house somewhere in a different part of the country where I don't want to be, but then I would have nothing left to live on and wouldn't be able to use any of my money to develop my work. *What's the point?* I questioned, *If I lose the chances I have gained?*

Suddenly this was turning into an exercise of recognising what I really valued and what mattered to me. It was about making choices. What did I want and what was I going to let go of? Who was I going to become?

Then the place started helping. I felt as though it was no longer just pulling me in but was actively starting to assist me in staying. "What do you need me to do, to stay here?" I asked it. "Merge with me," it replied. "You know you are of this place! Blend with it, not just occasionally but in every cell and breath. Fuse with the land and then you cannot leave because you will be part of it."

It's funny how things changed after I scattered the ashes. I'd never really considered the effect before I had to do it. I had to release something for new things to come. Maybe I should let go of some more things and see what happened. I made new friends. Usually because of Monty. The Monty effect was still as strong as ever. I met another local artist while we were both out with our dogs. One day I told her the story and as we stood looking across the field down to Caerthillian Cove, she said "Well, you've said it now! Put it out there and see what happens!" Immediately she spoke the words, a sparrowhawk lifted above the field edge and turned in the air over the waves of grass, right in my line of vision. A living omen. Subtle strokes of wings describing freedom upon the misty air. The sea breathed softly in our direction. Hawk led the way down the valley, to the margins of the land.

With the appearance of Sparrowhawk, I suddenly recalled a recurring dream, which has come to me many times in my life. In the dream I am always travelling somewhere, although the terrain and mode of travel may vary.

I become overly absorbed in some detail of finding my way. I look at everything around me and question which way is best; should I look at this? Or take that turning? Then something happens. I remember that I can lift myself up above the roads and fly. From the aerial viewpoint I can see further and better. I shapeshift into the form of a bird of prey.

With the realisation that I should be in the air, not on the ground, I pause. I recognise that I am dreaming. In the pause I breathe in and gather myself and as I breathe out, something within me draws upwards. It releases my sense of attachment to the ground. There is a distinct feeling, of uncurling upwards through my spine and another, of a form like wings, unfolding from my upper back and spreading to catch the wind. My legs diminish and fade.

I become bird. I lift upwards, high above the land. I observe the patterns in the sky. I scan the landscape below me, seeing for miles. Some places are brighter and others darker. I wonder which way to go. Then I spot the coastline. I move towards it, into that space where the sea and land meet. I am searching but it is unclear what for. A place? A way?

Given that I have dreamed this dream so many times, I was surprised I could have been so slow to comprehend that my inner self will always draw me back to the coast and has tried to tell me this often. Now, finally, I was remembering how to be myself again. It felt like a slow rebalancing of the inner and outer worlds.

"Use what you know," Hawk told me. "Be yourself, no matter what. You need very little to find your way, only the air and your own wings."

Chapter 29
Barefoot Child

Barefoot on the lawn, small pink toes wiggling among the grass and daisies. The earth was warm and felt delightfully alive under my feet. Just a few years old and I had already been barefoot in the garden for as long as I had been able to stand.

My mother, who taught me to walk my very first steps, allowed and encouraged me to do so barefoot at any opportunity. This wasn't a fashion or a health fad from some magazine. She would have had no time for such things. It was just what she thought sensible. She knew without having to be told that we need to grow with a sense of connectedness to the earth and that begins with sensing how we stand on it. Later on, when I was older, she told me that she had wanted me to grow with my feet feeling the earth.

I can readily recall many things about being a small baby. Like being around several months old, small enough to be picked up and carried in my mother's arms to bed, just able to reach out and push a light switch if she held me out towards it. I never forgot.

I still remember learning to stand up, crawling on the colourful woollen rugs on our living-room floor to the pieces of furniture that I could use to grab onto, pulling myself up to a standing position. I felt the change in awareness as it dawned on me that there was a world above me and if I stood up away from the patterned, woolly carpets I had been playing on, then I could begin to explore it.

One of my earliest memories is of being just about old enough to be barely able to stand, with my mother playing with me, holding my hands as I balanced and guiding me to stand up, with each one of my feet on top of each of hers. Then she would slowly walk backwards, laughing and encouraging, so that I could walk forwards on her feet without having to control my own legs, while I held onto her fingers, as she showed me how to put one foot in front of the other.

She showed me everything I needed to know, including how to respect the wild world, but most importantly she showed me how to stand on my own two feet and walk barefoot and unafraid.

I never liked wearing shoes and socks on my feet. My mum would put them on me to go out and as soon as I could, I would pull them off and toss them away so that I could wiggle my toes in the fresh air. Mum picked them up and I threw them away again. Apparently, I made quite a habit of it. Inside the house, when I was older, it was always my natural preference to be barefoot, if possible, even late into the autumn in cold weather.

From the moment I could walk, I went barefoot in the garden whenever I could. Wild was the sense of real earth under my feet. Knowing how to walk comfortably without having to think about it. Later, friends would see me barefoot and ask why I wasn't worried about walking on something sharp. The question seemed strange. It had never occurred to me because I just didn't do that. I wasn't concerned about it because I had learned without conscious effort to pay attention to where I was putting my feet.

Mum wasn't a clichéd Earth Mother type, she just said that she wanted to allow my feet to grow properly and for me to learn how to walk being able to feel the ground. She figured that out for herself, not from hearing or reading it somewhere. As a teenager, I took up karate. The classes were quite traditional and it came as second nature to me to train barefoot. I didn't have to re-learn how to balance without shoes on. My feet were already conditioned.

Empty hands and bare feet. To this day it is still my preference. I feel that when we walk barefoot, among other things, somehow, we honour the teachings of those who have been before us by connecting ourselves to the life journeys of our predecessors. It helps us learn to sense our place upon the earth when we feel it with our feet.

I walked barefoot in so many places as I grew up. Now it was time to do so again and it came as a reminder to keep growing and not become stale. I had learned to navigate life in the city, my feet on concrete walkways, hurrying between stations and meetings. Too long in shoes and boots had made my feet lose their familiarity with the ground, and with that loss, my very sense of physical balance had diminished.

But now, as I sought a fresh change of direction, there was no big, steady pair of hands to hold mine, no one to laugh and encourage and no larger, more experienced feet to stand on and show me how to find my steps. My feet have felt the colder since then and my heart smaller for the loss of my friend who first showed me how to walk.

Somewhere along that journey, I don't really remember how or when, I developed a fear of slipping that became quite intense. It started in my twenties or perhaps even earlier. It escalated. It became hard for me to walk down slopes without hesitating or feeling like I was going to slip over, even on the smallest gradients and quite reasonable surfaces. Ice, snow and slippery leaves all became stresses that left me needing extra time to walk even the shortest distance.

After twenty or so years, it had become bad enough that the challenge of walking on wet pavements left me shuffling along like an old woman, embarrassed to be seen that way and deliberately walking nearer to walls and railings so that I could reach out for security if I wanted to. London rushed by around me.

I, the barefoot fighter, once with the balanced and fluid movements, now struggled to walk down even a tiny incline. There was nothing wrong with me, I had just become scared and disconnected from the earth. I didn't take the time to stop and think why, I was too busy feeling under pressure to get where I needed to go, without anyone noticing the problem. Pavements which were wet to even the slightest degree left me nervous and clutching for support.

By the time I left London and my old life behind my body had become full of tension. Without a moment's delay I headed out onto the cliff path that I knew so well. It felt essential. I would have lived on this path if I could. Become like a mouse in the hedge or a hawk on the wind. At first, I felt like I was walking stiffly. I realised how hesitant my body had become.

But as soon as my feet touched the paths of reddish earth twining among the short turf and gorse, walking these trails felt automatically normal again as though I should never have left. Here, it was like this path and I were one. My balance began to return, as my awareness readapted itself. My feet know this track so well I could walk it with my eyes shut. My footfalls on the earth here have a slightly different sound and feel from anywhere else. This is home. When your bond with a place is so intimate that you could recognise it just from the unique qualities of your footsteps on that land, then how can it not be home?

There, I found myself questioning what that fear of falling had been about. I think sometimes the conditions we develop can be metaphors for our mind-talk which we have made real from what we have been telling ourselves. Every now and then when something in my body feels off-key, I like to ask myself what it represents. What phrases have I been using or listening to, which have taken shape this way?

I almost laughed aloud out there on the breezy coast path, when I realised the inner backdrop of mind-talk to which I had been listening for so long. The self-imposed judgement that I mustn't put a foot wrong. The fear of making mistakes and slipping up. Old memories of my mother talking about people going wrong, referring to them as "Going down the slippery slope!"

Oh shit! I thought. *We say things without thinking, but our bodies are listening all the time and they make it real!* The sea was starting to wash it all away in its music. All the mental detritus was dissolving into the tide and vanishing into unimportance, grain by grain. Just like the fire of the dragons in the Lake District, the transformative powers of the clear sea water flowed tangibly here. Flooding the air like the mist spreading over the land. Marine breezes carried the aromas of the ocean, touching the hedges and fields with enticements to explore.

Out on the high path across the clifftops, for decades, tiny trails of bare earth, cut by nothing more than footfalls, wove snakily through the short grass. Here, the red earth, exposed by footfalls, made soft, natural paths that wound along the cliffs in a cheerfully haphazard kind of way. 'Desire Lines' they are called. The little trails that form from the footfalls of people who have walked where their instincts and responses to the landscape took them.

Every year, the surrounding grass goes brown in late summer and the paths are at their most bare. Then autumn comes and with new rainfall the increased greening of the cliffs. The tracks change with the seasons but not over the years.

For over a quarter of a century I have been watching these trails and can honestly say they have not increased, eroded the terrain or caused damage to any greater extent in all that time. Every year they have ebbed and flowed slightly with the changing numbers of visitors through the seasons, but across that quarter-century span they have stayed the same.

Yet even here in this place of freedom the encroaching step of control creeps in. If our feet could write poetry, they would write in desire lines. Lyrical little interactions between feet and land. Humans and Places as one. The story of millennia, subtly described by the tempo of our feet.

This is not a damage or a detriment. The more significant change is being caused by those who interfere in the name of preservation. In an effort to stop people walking where they will and forming desire lines, some feel the need to make set paths. They call desire lines bad and say they erode the cliffs and damage the scenery. For them, desire lines are something to be controlled and constrained.

But they are missing the point. In etching their neatly chipped paths onto the clifftops, *they* damage the scenery. The desire lines here are part of the landscape and our interaction with it. People form them when they reconnect to the landscape in the act of moving freely. If they never experience their own footsteps on the earth, undictated by path or road, guided by nothing other than the shape of the land, inviting them, "Walk this way!" then they never learn how to move as one with their world. If people are not allowed to feel their connection to the land, they stop caring about it.

These twining lines follow the instinctive excitement of pursuing a natural trail, leading where nature guides us. The constructed paths, by contrast, are harsh underfoot and look unnatural here. Made from hard grey granite chippings grating against each other with an unpleasant crunch when walked upon, they have no place in this landscape.

The need to dictate and control how we interact with the wild had started encroaching even here, like the touch of some pervading will to keep people disconnected and unaware. The more I sensed that touch the more I wanted to flee from it. With my face to the breeze, barefoot with my dog, until we find a place where we can disappear into the land itself and nothing can pull us back into the unreal world.

I turned my back on the path of granite chippings and stayed in the wild. On those russet trails my feet knew the shape of the earth like some ancient, unwritten song. The old story, of which I am just a line. I walked where my feet and Monty's took us. I walked softly, in barefoot shoes, contemplating making moccasins so that I could walk more naturally in the wild. The desire line of my life had gone off on a trajectory at counterpoint to the common path and I felt blessed for the fact that it had. Here, above the blue sea, where the wall of air was like the touch of infinity, here the landscape matched the shape of my inner world. Is that how we know where our real home is? When the inner and outer worlds finally match?

I was starting to realise that this was about so much more than balance or walking. It was about reclaiming my right to be able to walk fearlessly. In the wild and in life. Reclaiming my wild-self who could put one foot in front of the other with natural confidence and ease. I took off my shoes and walked the trail without them. I cooled my toes in the stream that ran through the valley and enjoyed the freshness. I walked all the way back unshod, remembering myself and the sense of how my body wanted to walk.

Chapter 30
Beach

The remembering grew. All was interwoven now. Time was thinner here. Solid matter seemed more transparent somehow. I went to Kennack Sands and there I heard the voice of my mother amid the bird calls and surf, saying, "Take your shoes off!" Shingle rustled in the curling waves.

Awakening stirred with every whisper. I yanked off my footwear and stood with the cool water flowing around my ankles. Wet sand seeping between my toes was an adventure of rediscovery. "Feel how you stand!" the earth told me. "Feel the ground through your feet." Every tiny shift of those countless grains under the touch of my feet, like moments, asked for my awareness. The movements called upon my feet to relax.

Hey! I'm standing on my own two feet! I'd been going through life thinking I was, but really all those things which are supposed to assist us just weaken us. I stood, like Monty, with bare feet on the sand, the pull of the tide tugging at our ankles, fanning his soft black fur in the clear water and sparkling across my skin. Truly standing on my own two feet. Nothing but us, our connection to the earth and sky.

"I will honour everything you taught me!" I had promised my mother as she was dying. Now I told her again, casting my words to the horizon and hoping she would hear them. "I will share it with others and you will know that what you gave me has gone on, perhaps even around the world." That promise echoed in every ripple on the tide, as I stood barefoot on the beach amid the pools of clear water, weeping sorrow and joy for the entwined transience and power of life.

"I will honour everything you taught me," I told her, there in the running tide. "Let my bare footedness be my tribute to your bravery and intuitive wisdom. Let all my journeys honour the start you gave me. May my words convey your hopes and insights across oceans and years. I am your barefoot child. I will remember you forever."

Monty seemed to understand. Whether on the beach, in the fields, or the high trails, his four little paws padded along beside mine, in a contented kind of way. Regardless of what I might have lost or what I might be looking for, all he asked was to come too. A barefoot child. A nomad with my dog at my side. With Monty I was no longer lost but travelling.

I fell more deeply into moments. I returned little by little to the wild space, the infinite wild, the flow of life. Golden sunlight glanced onto the sea through feathery clouds. With each wave, the tide drew me in a little closer to reality. The surf-line became a sort of doorway from which I was reluctant to retreat. I had to be close to it. It clarified things. It dispelled illusion. There is something about the sea which simplifies everything. Wherever I walk, whichever life paths I turn to, it is always the sea that calls me back to its shores.

"You can't live out here on a cliff!" screamed Logic. "Be quiet!" I told Logic. "Perhaps I can't, but I can't live without it either." If 'home' isn't a place, then what is it? What is it to a nomad? Is 'home' a state of being? What is home but a state of inner knowledge? Maybe home is within ourselves. Maybe it is our connectedness to life to which we return. Maybe the skill of the nomad is to perfect the state of constantly returning to the wild.

I remembered the older, wiser me I had been when I was younger. When waking dreams were part of each day and the spirit of flight was as easy as walking, as it is before we become heavy with fear and doubt. I started to remember being her. The way I did before the unwild world intervened. Something was growing stronger within me, a patch of green grass, given fresh air and rain. I might not have a home of my own, but I was thriving on having space to grow. "I think I'll make moccasins!" I spontaneously told Monty, as I tickled his ears.

Midwinter came again and before the turn of the morning tide, the first light found me on the beach with Monty. The tide was running strong and a storm had passed overnight, blowing away with the rising of the sun. A man was walking along the beach, in my direction though not aiming specifically towards me. "Good morning!" I greeted him as he drew closer. "Good morning," he replied.

It was unusual to encounter someone there in the winter, in the early hours of the morning, particularly if they were not with a dog. But somehow, he seemed to fit. A part of the landscape, like a seagull on a rock. Grey hair, the colour of beach pebbles. Blue eyes, with hints of light reminiscent of reflected sun on waves and the shadows of submerged rocks. A battered hat and a walking stick which was more of a staff that he did not appear to need to aid him in walking. 'And good morning to you!' he greeted and petted Monty, who responded delightedly with the kind of enthusiasm he normally saved for extra-special friends.

We spoke for a few short minutes. An eternity passed. The Universe blinked. Two conversations unfolded simultaneously. One spoken and one wordless. Of the spoken one I cannot recall a word that was said between good morning and goodbye. The other is hard to express.

The Universe turned a fraction and like a kaleidoscope the colours of my thoughts shifted. Each one tumbling against the next and setting off a chain reaction of colours which started here but would only unfold over the coming weeks. The world breathed in and then paused. Something timeless and wordless passed between us in the space of a heartbeat. Not years but lifetimes of experience compressed into moments and shared between us in an instant of something clearer than explanations and purer than thought.

Then the world breathed out again. We wished each other well. He walked away, eastwards in the direction of the serpentine rocks which divide the two beaches and the coast path leading to Coverack. As time started to flow outwards from the moment, I felt inexplicably compelled to look at a spot on the ground. Two flattish stones, the size of my hand, magnetically pulled my gaze. One, graphite in colour, was scored all over with criss-crossing, rune-like white lines. Some clear and others fainter, suggesting old inscriptions worn half smooth by the waves and tumbling of pebbles.

The other held no immediately obvious reason to attract me, yet it spoke clearly, "Pick me up!" I did so and turned it over in my hands. It felt alive. It was interestingly marked, diagonally, into rough halves, part grey and part white, yet still I could not see why this stone out of so many thousands. What was special about it? "Stop trying to see with your eyes," it told me. I walked to the tide line and stood there, turning it around and raising it to the rising sun. Immediately, the light and dark tones took on the shape of a wolf's face. I held a stone to the rising light, yet I was looking into the face of a wolf and there on the edge of the sea, a wolf looked back.

Wolf-stone in my hands and dog at my side, I looked along the edge of the waves towards the rising sun. The man was nowhere in sight. The moment hung suspended in the eyes of eternity. Doorways of possibility opened. A tiny hoverfly flickered at the corner of my thoughts. The memory of a dream re-opened, parting confining hedges with my hands, to emerge into sunlit fields. Red kites dancing, calling me to make beauty with my hands.

I opened my heart a little wider in honour of wild things. I thanked the beach for bringing me the stranger and the stones. I kissed Monty, grateful for him bringing me to the beach. I celebrated myself a little more and all the journey that had brought me here. All those who shared it on my way. Before the wind and waves, I had come a little closer to home. A wolf on the shore of the sea. Part of the place.

Chapter 31
The Nomad's Hearth

Self-doubts and fears of risk-taking bombarded me like hailstones at every twist and turn. "You're being unrealistic!" I criticised myself almost every day, to which a stronger, more stubborn side of me would calmly reply, "So, who gets to decide what realistic is anyway?"

A memory of a tiny golden hoverfly slipped into my thoughts, as if in affirmation; translucent wings flickering in approval. A little shining messenger, reminding me that we are all dreaming and if I am dreaming then it is my dream, so I choose what is real. I will dream myself as an author and artist with a home in the fields which run down to the cliffs above the sea. I focus upon it, the place I have seen in my dreams for years. I know it is real. It sits near a headland, with a small gate at the bottom of the garden that leads out to a path that runs to the sea.

The sea! It doesn't sound the same here as anywhere else. I've been on beaches all around this country and some elsewhere in the world, but the sea sounds different here in the High Place. Someone else might just hear waves but when I stand in this place, I feel it in the centre of my chest. Something in me matches it and I know that I am home. But what defines the sound of the sea? The weather, certainly, but it sounds different here in any weather. So, what makes that? Does the physical shape of the coast have something to do with it? The type of rock that the waves meet and the angle of contact, defined by the shape of the sea floor? Is it the fact of being lifted up above it on the cliffs? The joining of land, sky and sea. Or is it something else? Something stranger? Is this what the voice of home sounds like?

I don't know. But I believe that if someone made audio recordings of the sea, from locations all around this country, and played them to me blindfold, with no other sensory cues, I would know which one was recorded here.

The inner nomad knows that onward movement is essential. Without the capacity to leave a place and move on, reading the signs that change is on the horizon and doing nothing is to risk being caught in a storm, or the approach of winter. At the season's turn, the nomad does not go back. Our ancestors followed their experience and the messages of nature. Now, we may not need to gather and hunt in order to survive, but we can still die inwardly.

If I went back now to anywhere else that I had been before, it would feel like ignoring those cues. True that I had been in Cornwall many times before but it never felt static. To live here on the Lizard was constant renewal. With every breath I felt life rising afresh through my being. I had brought Mum's ashes here and I knew now why she had asked. She may never have put the reason into words but she didn't need to. Light is brighter here, life is stronger. Nothing stands still. There is no need to move because here everything is in constant movement.

I wanted to spend every moment as close to that path as possible. Out there, I can always feel the spin of the world. Away at the curve of the horizon, all is possible. Earth hangs suspended in its place in the Universe and from there circle within circle unfolds around me. Planet within galaxy. Orbit the sun. Shell on the beach. Perfect spiral in my hand mirrors the galaxy. From my palm new worlds unfold. Layer within layer. Who knows what may be?

And so, I am here again. Here in this curving, twisting universe. Here by the field corner, noticing the curves of the leaves, the tempo of rain. Breathing again. Here in the real world. The hedges, gorse-thick, full of blackthorn and ferns, uncurl all the way from the fields to the sea. You can see reality unfolding and unfurling in every direction. Converging. This place is magic. This is where spirit can touch freedom. The land whispers that the magic we are born of flows through everything, including us.

Logic and fear challenge, "You cannot stay here!" But Soul screams, "Don't send me back!" So, I listen to Soul and dare to ask it, "If I'm staying… then how?"

Strange how asking a slightly different question changes the answers you give yourself. Your whole outlook alters from there. Doorways open because you see them for the first time and the nomad has new paths to explore. You take your dog for a walk at a different time, or you say hello to a stranger in a battered hat. Your mind shifts and in the blink of an eye paths appear at your feet.

Into the Whispering Wild

I

I am the white-pebble finder, set free.
I am the barefoot wanderer me.
I am the lover of mist and rain,
Discovering the magic I was born from, again.

Trail finder, rain-dancer, out in the wild,
Owl watcher, beachcomber, pagan child.
I walk with a wolf to the gate between worlds.
I lift up to the sky as my wings unfurl.

I am oak leaf upon the wind.
I am the dancing skylark's friend.
I am the sparkle of light on the sea,
Following the Wild Mystery

Holder of wolf-stone on the seashore.
Guardian keeper of ancient lore.
I walk with my dog where the worlds meet.
I learn from the sand shifting under our feet.

Writer of stories I learn from the wild.
Traveller among the misty isles,
I fly with Hawk where the sky is wide.
I walk in the light where worlds coincide.

'Staying' is a word which is strange to the nomad. But here it makes a different kind of sense. If all the world is moving, made up of elements which are moving, within a universe in which all parts are in motion, am I not moving even if I appear to stay still? Is it not impossible for any physical body to be still? I can stand motionless in one spot on the planet but together we are still spinning through space.

I write beside the log burner. The February nights are still cold. I have come to think of my fire as the nomad's hearth. Winter has passed and March is almost upon us. Every time I think the storms have abated another crashes in. If weather could be a metaphor for our lives, then this winter mirrors the last two years of my life to perfection. Every time I can take a breath of stability I am tossed by another gale.

I'm ready for spring now. More than ready. As if in answer, sunlight starts to gain strength. The sky clears, one pale little cerulean patch at a time. What is this place trying to tell me? The struggle is of my own making. Gifts are everywhere. I look at the gifts and I refuse to fear. I reject negative anger, guilt, self-recrimination. It makes no sense but I do it anyway. I ask for inspiration and direction. Life gives me sea glass and unexpected friends. I take Monty for a walk in the fields and get soaked by the strengthening downpours before we get back. Wrapping Monty in a towel I hang my sodden clothes over the log burner, relishing the warmth of the golden flames. A raw-edged wind is gathering swiftly outside.

Barely have I finished changing my clothes when there is a quiet knock at the door. I open it to be greeted by a mouth-watering waft, rising on the steam from a plate of hot food. Like a good fairy materialising by magic, my friend Judy tentatively offers me a plate of fragrant curry, asking shyly, 'Would you like this?' The aromas of citrus and spice fill the caravan with deliciousness. I would rather have eaten that gift of home-made curry than any banquet on earth. It smelled and tasted exquisite and the timing was perfection.

The following morning, we go to the beach. The tide is running high, frothing across the shingle in steady surges. Barely a couple of feet of sand left before it begins crashing at the foot of the low cliff. We contemplate taking the other way around on the top path, but in front of us through the surf it is only a few short, splashy yards to the wider part of the beach. We have time, and the most we risk is soggy socks *if* we don't hesitate. "We can do it if we go *now*!" I declare. I wait for the wave to recede and then run at the gap. We rush through the foaming water, laughing and invigorated.

Judy looks at me, wide-eyed and glowing like an excited child. I run for it and she follows, laughing. As soon as I move, the dogs are ahead of us, leaping and dancing through the circling waves. They reach the wide part in seconds and chase each other playfully, scattering sand and surf with their paws as they dash gleefully up the beach. "Move on without hesitation!" the beach taught me. "Move when you see your chance."

This whole place is a metaphor. I suddenly understand. Life speaks in metaphors but it is clearer here somehow. We run on the sand like children, play with the dogs, watch them paddle in the stream from the woods. We smell the air and laugh together, immersing ourselves in this Place, sometimes literally! The wild is talking in its own language. The language of bird, animal, tree and element. Now I know what Chief Seattle meant. They are all lines in the same song. As are we.

As night falls, Monty rests close to me. The bond of life between us, vibrant and enriching. It deepens daily, uninterrupted, untainted. Perfection is listening to his breathing when he sleeps next to me. Simplicity and love.

Part 7
The Adventure

"It doesn't interest me what you do for a living. I want to know what you ache for and if you dare to dream of meeting your heart's longing. It doesn't interest me how old you are. I want to know if you will risk looking like a fool for love, for your dream, for the adventure of being alive."

The Invitation, Oriah Mountain Dreamer

Chapter 32
Beyond Reason

I walk with Monty through fields of long grass, angling diagonally towards a spot where the land starts to drop into a valley that descends to the sea. Across the hedges and trees, I can see out to the meeting point of land and tide. I wander along, worrying about things like finding somewhere to live and watching Monty enjoying following scents along the hedgerows.

I've been beating myself up for days wondering how I got into this mess and suddenly, in the rain-washed field, I know why I need to stop. I remember I have been in this exact situation before. How could I have forgotten that? Is time like some sort of tide, which washes some things away and brings others back later to the shore, at a moment of its choosing?

Just over twenty years earlier, I had decided that my life wasn't working out. I had been sitting in a house I was renting, with a business that I shared with Robin, but neither of us really knew how to make work. I was descending into a tide of mental fog that was threatening to drown me. Every day I got up and the same worries were there. It became paralysing. Until one day I asked myself a different question, a wonderful question which I will always remember because I had based my next steps upon it and that foundation changed everything for the better. The question was this: "If there was one thing, for which you would change everything, even if you don't yet know how; one thing for which you would be willing to take a first step into uncertainty, when you don't yet know your way, what would it be?"

I had known the answer then. What I would do it for. Acting

upon that knowledge had changed my life immeasurably for the better, leading me eventually through a maze of decisions to a good, rewarding career, financial stability, great colleagues and amazing friends. Once I had known that answer I could take steps towards finding out how to achieve it. What I didn't know, I could learn. From there, I could organise my thoughts and it had been easy to discover each step I needed to take.

What is the answer to that question now? I feel as though I have lived a lifetime since then and in some ways I have. With the memory comes confidence. I have been through this before and made it work out well. I can do so again. It's just a cycle of renewal. A country child, I had left the place I grew up in for love. Robin and I had gone to Kent together, full of hope and naivety. In time, the stress of wondering how to make a living and achieve our dreams combined with all that we didn't know and it tore us apart. Well, it tore me apart, mentally, and I left, heading to the city, and followed a path into the grey world. We stayed friends. We had put things back together after a fashion because the love was still there. The unreal world had just piled too much shit on top of us for me to be able to see beyond it to what mattered.

I always wished I'd never left. That I had known enough to see our way through together without going. But sometimes you just don't know what you don't know. Then you find you can't go back. Somehow the road changes us. Sometimes the roads of Earth only take us so far. We spent one beautiful afternoon together, as if we had never been apart. We walked in Greenwich Park, playing with squirrels and giving them funny names, before spending the rest of the day in bed. Then I went back to my part of the illusion and he to his.

I guess we always thought we'd have more time. I had no idea I had seen him for the last time. Then I got a call to say he'd died. Just one call, when I was on a train. A short, resentful call from a judgemental relative who excluded me from his memorial service because we had separated and she didn't want me around. I hardly heard her words after she spoke the first news. They faded behind a stark wall of shock and pain. A chest infection had turned to pneumonia and triggered complications from a long-term health condition which we had always known could shorten his life but somehow never believed would do. Then I couldn't go back, because there were no more roads to follow which could bring us together, save one. Maybe, one day, it will.

Back then as I took the first slow steps through the marsh of uncertainty, I was traversing a much darker terrain than where I now find myself. Then I had next to nothing in the bank, some hopes and plans, a job in a coffee shop and a rented room in a shared student house near a junction in Deptford. I couldn't even get back into the address in the evening without having to evade a gang of feral youths, who spread out across each of the street corners taking up positions there, waiting for people to mug.

I would carefully walk the entire way around the extremities of the junction and cross four extra roads to avoid their net. Now, I can step outside with Monty and head into the fields. The only things outside in the evening here are owls, moths and bats. I don't have to dodge muggers. The most challenging risk my environment presents now is not slipping over in the mud. I might be in the marsh of uncertainty once more, but at least now I have an inner map and some good friends I've met along the way. I smile when I realise that I'm going around the same loop but on a different level and how much better things have become. I haven't messed up. I am on a twenty-year cycle of renewal. It was a great question before, so what happens if I ask it again? What would I step into the unknown for this time?

The answer is clear. I would do it to be the writer and artist I've always wanted to be, living close to the cycle of the year happily with my dog. I would do it to write about the wild and share what it tells me. To live in Lys Ardh and be part of this place for as long as life allows me to, expressing its wild beauty, to inspire others. Success? Am I allowed that too, or is that asking too much? Are the only limits my expectations? When I get indoors, I log into my Instagram account and a friend has posted about butterflies, "If you want to attract butterflies, don't run around chasing them, plant a garden!" You attract things by being who you are, I realise, not just what you do. Authenticity is powerful. I set out to attract the butterflies to my garden.

Now I can start to plan again because I have something to work with. I plan with every fibre of my spirit, plucking thoughts and ideas and starting to twist them together into a creative process of hope. I draw the threads of hedge and field, yarrow and nettle, bramble and vetch. I call upon birdsong and the depths of the sea. I weave them into the shape of my life as I release my remaining mind from its last shackles and let it lead me, instead of trying to contain it. I am starting to realise that it is the whole process of creating which I am learning to extend from paintings and books to writing the pages of real life itself.

The lyrical land speaks in hues of bracken and gorse. My eyes become more attuned to textures in the land and each little feature shows me something new. Here a curled leaf, there a footprint. A soft cobweb, drenched in dew. A glint of quartz, shining on the path. Reflected light everywhere, a pervading, soundless song.

"Is this magic?" I ask the sky. "To weave the path unfolding? The fabric of our lives?" The sea surges in response, "It is the magic you were born to know." The sky speaks back, "That life is yours to weave. The wild will share its ideas, patterns and colours with you in abundance. If you let it. Weave with threads of wave and surf, of wind, cloud, sun and mist. Tell your fellow humans to look to the wild for their inspiration too and respect it. For if they do not, then for every bird that ceases to sing, every stream that stops running because it is dammed or polluted and every tree cut down, their lives will be the poorer. Each time a part of the wild disappears from this world, it is one thread less your race can weave with, one thread less in your knowledge of life and the fabric of your lives will be weaker."

"What shall I weave?" I ask the sea.

"Weave the life you want!" it tells me. "Your kind has been asking me about life for as long as you have walked this earth. But you, *you* have cut the threads on the loom. The weave of events which would have been if you had stayed where you were, are now lost to mystery. You'd better learn to weave well!" A single word keeps blocking my path, surfacing like a giant sea-serpent from the depths. I voice it to the sea; "But it's impossible!" I call disconsolately. "Impossible!"

"No wonder you're exhausted!" the sea mocks me lightly with its effortless power. "If you keep doing battle with that old monster. Why do you humans keep dragging 'Impossible' up from the deep? No wonder it's always cross! Is it not time to let the poor thing have some rest and try 'Possible' instead?"

I sit on a rock with Monty and listen to the sea. "Do you know all my depths?" it sighs. "Once, people who knew less about what is on the surface of the earth than you do, managed to cross entire oceans before they knew their way. When they pulled on the oars and sails of the first ships and looked at the stars, do you think they ever felt that it was impossible to find land? Of course they did. So, what did they do? Do you think they just stopped there, halfway across and decided that because it seemed impossible, they had better just let themselves drown?"

I understand now. I am not going to drown. I refuse to let myself give up on everything I came this far for. What am I going to weave? If I am a weaver of life, I must choose only the very best threads. Because this is not a garment I will eventually wear out. The fabric of my life is all I will eventually leave behind to show others. Maybe someone can use it as a chart to cross an ocean of their own.

I throw away doubt and replace it with creativity. I dump recrimination and actively feed my sense of gratitude. I discover that gratitude has amazing power. When I feel angry that I don't have enough space in my cooking area and a proper kitchen, I try being grateful that I have food to cook and my mother had shown me how to make hot meals. When I feel upset that the caravan windows run with condensation in the cold, I am grateful that I have a solid roof over my head keeping the rain out and a fire to sit beside. Instead of being irritated that the tap drips I am grateful to have running water.

Strange things start to happen. My backache vanishes, the sore spot on my gum heals without me trying to treat it. From that moment I practise gratitude with a fervour, not because of any goody-two-shoes idealism, but because it is empowering!

I turn my attention to the hardest one, the mind-monster that most threatens to stop me in my tracks, the spectre of fear. When I want to write books, it is fear more than anything else that seems able to freeze me into submission. Fear would send me running back to the false world where I can fit in with all its expectations and apologetically pretend that I had never tried to be something more.

Fear is paralysing. It destroys creativity. If I bow to fear I will never follow the path I have set my feet upon or the knowledge my mother instilled in me years ago. It would disrespect her gifts. Fear would dishonour the faithful dog who walks beside me every day and teaches me to see the wild. Fear that my choices will not work out would lead me to become angry at my decisions and resentful of my hopes and dreams. That is the path to a darkness which yawns in front of me every time I feel afraid. Suddenly, the words of Yoda in *Star Wars, The Phantom Menace*, have never been truer or more empowering, "Fear is the path to the dark side. Fear leads to anger. Anger leads to hate. Hate leads to suffering."

So, I pour light upon my fears. It's a choice. Starlight in the night sky and firelight in the hearth. The light in my dog's eyes conveys enough love to transmute anything, even the darkest demon. The path of light across the sea from the High Place. Midsummer light, midwinter light. Light shining on a hoverfly's wings. All the light from the candles I have ever lit to mark the turning seasons. I light more candles, for hope, for those I have lost, for the belief that they aren't lost and are watching the light I send them. Because anything is better than fear.

Any time I open a box in my mind which holds something I am afraid of, I consciously open the doorway to light and carry it through, like ashes to be released. Past the random lamp post on the cliffs which marks the entrance to the High Place and out to where my soul meets the wild. Because there, everything looks different.

The elements do not fear. Does the sea fear the sky just because each day water evaporates? No, it surrenders itself to the air, allowing itself to be carried to places it could not otherwise reach, to fall again as rain and start the journey home. Released like a caged eagle, escaping from some inner place where I keep inspirational quotes and soaring to the front of my thoughts with all the flair of a superhero to the rescue, come the lines by Frank Herbert in his work *Dune*:

"I must not fear. Fear is the mind-killer. Fear is the little death that brings total obliteration. I will face my fear. I will permit it to pass over me and through me. And when it has gone past, I will turn the inner eye to see its path. Where the fear has gone there will be nothing. Only I will remain."

I make it my mantra. I force myself to make fear ridiculous. I take it to the point of absurdity until I just have to find it funny, so that I can laugh at my fears – and move on from them, breaking the inertia.

My bank balance is dwindling – I will not fear!
I can't afford somewhere to live – I will not fear!
I might not be able to stay in the Lizard – I will not fear!
I haven't kept all my paperwork up to date – I will not fear!
I live in a caravan – I will not fear!
I've got to pay my car off – I will not fear!
I'm overwhelmed with uncertainty – I will not fear!
I'm getting older – I will not fear!
I've spilt my coffee everywhere – Oh, this is ridiculous! I will not fear!
Bollocks, now I've run out of coffee – OK, I'm going to the shop!
Back to thinking about money again. But I will not fear!
I WILL NOT FEAR!

My work changes. My paintings become looser and more alive in feeling. Quietly and with focus, I weave the threads of a new life. I pull together the strands of softly gleaming sea glass, with dancing skylarks, twisting serpentine paths and deep green lanes. Blackthorn and bracken. Buzzards soaring above the strip of heathland, edging the line of the rugged cliffs. Seagulls skimming over the waves. Hope effortlessly replaces worry. Not all the time, but often. I weave with words and colours on paper, canvases and the pages of my books. With pens and paints. They stop being separate. They flow into each other. Monty looks at me with hopeful, enthusiastic eyes and fetches a ball for us to play with.

Chapter 33
Winds of Change

The winter blows over us and away, with one last frantic windstorm in March, then finally subsides into mildness and showers. Sunshine peeps out for the odd day here and there, starting to gather strength. I feel the cycle of the year and with the growing light I too begin to grow stronger once more.

I walk out onto the path, sharing the celebration of spring gales with the soaring gulls and pale golden sun. Everything is saturated from constant rain, but the welcome light is increasing each day and with it, I find I breathe more easily. Everywhere, there are birds. The bushes are alive with tiny brown wrens, hopping out of the branches, and peeking at me shyly before whizzing off. Blue tits hang from the window frames and tap cheekily on the glass. Clog- dancing wood pigeons clatter around enthusiastically upon the roof, cooing and flapping. Chaffinches rattle and ping from the tops of the apple trees.

My inner self screams from behind a straitjacket of mind-fog. So, I listen to it and give myself permission to wander in nature instead. Why have I been making myself think unnaturally? When did that start? I allow my brain to think however it wants to. As I do, I notice more wild things. My brain had been trying to do this all along. Maybe the reason I couldn't think straight is because we aren't supposed to. Our thought processes are not meant to be railroaded into the rigidly straight forms that so many of our modern cultures demand of us.

We didn't always think in lines and boxes. We are born of the natural world. We are not creatures of straight lines. We were not born to live lives of inflexibility. There is a space within where thought, feeling and spirit merge. Trees now thick with green leaves wave and toss in the wind. Fire kindles again in the evening hearth. This accidental nomad is putting down roots. Or perhaps coming to understand that in Places of magic, motion and stillness coincide.

I stand on the cliff path. Skylarks whirl around by day and stars spin overhead by night. The wild storms and vast rainbows describe my life. Tossed and hammered, windswept but hanging on, giant leaps of hope illuminate my world and clear my inner vision. Slowly, storm by storm, the inner pool clears a little more.

I wish on each one of those sparkling arcs to bring me home. Home to stay. Here I know what home is. Here, I wonder how I could have ever thought I didn't know. Once I am here, there is no longer any doubt in my mind. Here it is a certainty that makes me ask how I could question it. But once I go away, I just feel lost. Home becomes a hope that I start to doubt I can find my way back to. Like a memory of Avalon, which leaves me unsure whether I can part the mists to find my way back.

In this place, the sense of home is bone-deep. The land pulses with a tangible current of something hard to explain, like electricity but more refined. My whole being resonates to it, like strings in the same chord where each vibrates when the other is plucked. It rises from the ground. Nowhere else have I felt that the same way. I have always sensed the spirit of a place, the power of the land. I have travelled the United Kingdom literally from side to side and end to end, but nowhere else does my soul respond to Place the way it does here. Everything from the voices of my ancestors and my mother's spirit, to my gut and my dog, all say, "Stay here!" But how? How do I cut through the fog of illusions of what I think I can have and weave this life?

The critic within still says I am being unreasonable. The truer self who I am becoming responds, "I'm done with reasonable. At least with the kind of reasonable that's just an excuse for believing our own shadows. Fuck reasonable!" Life isn't reasonable so why should I be? Wild isn't reasonable. You have to be unreasonable to survive and I need to survive as my real self, not some half-baked interpretation of it. It isn't natural to reason with life. I am caught somewhere between optimism and stubbornness. Why shouldn't I be where I want to? There's no universal rule that says I can't. It's up to me to discover what is possible.

Spring is whispering from every hedgerow. Daffodils have been in flower for weeks here. Vivid pink camellia bushes have been in full bloom, completely unreasonably, since January. Or it would be unreasonable anywhere else, but here it seems perfectly sensible, in keeping with the magic of the place. Every twig on every tree is budding. I refuse to fear. I cannot fear uncertainty in a place where the first daffodil opens on Midwinter's Day. It didn't worry about whether it was allowed to open and flower that day, or whether it was too early. It just bloomed. Brilliant yellow, dazzling boldness in the darkest point of winter.

I'm done with excusing what I want. I refuse to be an apologist for my dreams for one moment longer. I belong here! I might be stupid enough to have travelled all around the United Kingdom looking for alternatives, only to figure out that this is the only place that makes me truly happy and I feel homesick as soon as I leave, but I don't have to carry on that way. I can trust my inner knowing instead.

What is it that makes us 'of a place'? What makes us belong somewhere? It isn't being born there. I was born in Essex but familiarity does not always equal affinity. Essex mostly felt like just another place to me. It was home for a while, but it wasn't home. It has green country fields, twisting lanes and thick hedges that taught the childhood me how to understand the wild world. But if anyone asks me where I am from, I struggle to say that I am from Essex, because I have no sense of connection to it. Parts of it are beautiful, I just never belonged there. I was born there, I grew up there, both these things are true, but to be a part of a place implies something more, which I have never experienced anywhere but in Cornwall. I may not be 'from Cornwall' but we are linked in a way that is beyond all normal explanations.

There is a layer of perception, a flat plane of experience, which some people dwell in and never leave. It defines their world and they perpetuate it because they have never considered living outside it, or even that there could be anything else. I don't know a name for it, so I am going to call it The Maboroshi - the Japanese word for illusion. People fall into it sometimes and struggle to get out because they don't know they are in an illusion. But the people we think we are when we are there, they are not us. We are more than that. The lives we live there seem real and compelling, but they are not the total of our experience or potential, they are stories.

Many things exist within the Maboroshi. Things which are real only for the effect they have in this unreal place. Yet within it, they have power. Real because we make them so. But that means they need us. Without us they would have no power so they befuddle our senses with entertainment, media and marketing distractions. Until we become so dependent we all but completely forget the instincts which tell us there is a world outside. One we were all born knowing. The creations of our minds have become real and they need us to keep feeding them with our attention so that they stay real.

The wild isn't welcome in the Maboroshi, other than as something to be exploited for more money. Nothing is welcome there which empowers people to withdraw their energy from it. It grimly strips people of everything natural that gives them resilience, independent comfort and self-knowledge. Ancient knowledge is scoffed at in this half-world. Herbal remedies and healing traditions are politely labelled 'alternative' or vilified as fraudulent. People who can think for themselves, produce their own food and the basic staples of life are frowned upon as 'weirdos.'

This is not the world of mountains, trees or ocean winds, but of politics, economies and stock markets, internet and ideologies. These things aren't intrinsically bad but what is bad is keeping people trapped in illusion, like prisoners in a hall of mirrors, wandering among reflected images and never stepping outside into daylight. Losing the ability to tell the difference between what is real and what isn't.

The world is falling into the grip of people who think only in terms of profit margins not roadside margins. In their world, people who think independently or self-sufficiently become persecuted. If things continue as they have been, those who hold onto the old knowledge are going to be portrayed as every bit as much of a problem as they were in witch hunts during the Dark Ages. A polarisation is beginning to form between people who want to escape the Maboroshi, who sense a way out, and others who are so much a part of it that they don't want to hear anything which tells them otherwise. As long as the dream is acceptable, even if not pleasant, then sometimes it is easier to stay asleep.

The wild whispers freedom. Land, sea, wind and rain knew who we were before the illusions started to take hold of us. The wind blows fresh showers, scattering raindrops on the caravan windows and bringing a sense of invigorating newness. When will the winds of change blow?

An inexplicable exhaustion keeps pouring itself over my senses. Shedding it feels like trying to throw off a blanket of industrial-grade treacle. Every time I fight my way out from under a corner of it, a different bit envelops me and sticks to my awareness. What is this? Where does it come from? It feels like a deadening of wakefulness. I sense the wings of Sky Dragon soaring through the dusk, riding on a spring storm. "Use the gift! Use the fire!" I turn back within myself to the inner fire and unleash it on the mental fog.

Whenever we leave rigid or controlling frameworks behind, we have to re-adapt. Our brains have to learn how to think again in ways they would have done if we had never been captive. 'Shock of capture' is the term which describes the experience of hostages when the brain freezes after being taken captive. Disorientation temporarily overwhelms thought when the free are deprived of liberty. But it does the same when freedom is suddenly the province of those who have never known it before.

So familiar are we with our cages that sometimes we don't notice the walls which confine us. The time when we were free was generations earlier. So accustomed are we to imprisonment now that we go into shock when we escape. So why does no one ever talk about the shock of 'un-capture' which comes with freedom? A jolt of aliveness awakens us to the lessening of captivity when we start to extricate ourselves from the mask of the unreal. Cages fade away and we realise that they were of our own making. We start to feel our own potential stirring.

Self-determination is a right we applaud but we validate it with one hand while simultaneously undermining it with the other. I am not free, exactly, but certainly un-captured and working on the rest.

Chapter 34
Sea Glass and Driftwood

The beach is full of magic and messages. In every pebble, the Universe is speaking. The breeze sings across the waves, full of stories of dolphins and distant shores. A large grey seal pops his head above the water and turns a wet, whiskery nose my way, watching with curious regard. I play with Monty and I hope for a home of my own. Somewhere safe to live and work. I just want to be able to get up in the morning, take Monty to the beach, or out in the fields, and get on with a day's work doing what I love. Otherwise, what have I done all this for? Why travel all around the UK trying to convince myself to live somewhere else, only to come back to the same part of the country because I can't stay away, if I'm not going to have the sense to listen to myself?

Seal waves a lazy flipper at me and blows air out through his whiskery nostrils, with a small wet sigh that I can almost feel from the shore. He makes me laugh. "Don't worry," Seal tells me. "Just play more! When I'm looking for something, I hunt in the seaweed. That's a good place to find nice things!"

"Thanks, Seal!" I call to him. "That's good advice."

When I listen to the sea around the Lizard, I hear something else, something hard to define. Like an ageless silence that sits behind the sound, yet somehow has a substance and a voice of its own. Like the darkness of night sky between the stars, you see nothing but know the Universe has a shape much larger than the details we can see. A space in which there may be other stars, unseen by our eyes. It's like hearing that vast distance. The sea-voice is constant yet somehow there is a much larger voice behind it. Vast, empty, yet full. Silently full-voiced.

Somehow the potential of hope seems enormous when you find that you can hear the Universe.

I discover the wonder of sea glass. Jewel-bright colours or ice-cube white, fragments of glass, tumbled smooth, worn and frosted by decades, sometimes even hundreds of years, in the sea until they wash up on the shoreline. Once I see the first, clear piece among the pebbles, searching for it becomes an inspiration. On an entire beach of grey pebbles, when you look closer there are these sparkles of colour waiting to be discovered. Frosted surfaces, subtly shining, worn smooth by the motion of the waves over time.

Sea glass teaches me to change perspective. The first time someone told me that there was a lot of sea glass here, I was surprised. I'd never seen any. I looked and looked, but still found none. Then one morning, while Monty and I are playing ball, he runs back to me ball in mouth and drops it. When I bend down to pick it up, shining next to it is a beautiful, rounded nugget of clear, frosted glass. I look closer and find three other pieces in that immediate patch of shingle. It had been there all along, I just hadn't been seeing it. But once I can see it, I see it everywhere! On the same morning that I find that first piece, I collect another twenty, within an hour.

Sea glass becomes my way of remembering to delight in the discovery of randomness and unexpected beauty. Apart from an abundance of white and all different shades of green, I find pale aqua, teal, red, orange, brown, olive, cornflower blue, pure ultramarine and even a tiny fragment of lavender. Little gifts from the sea.

Things we thought we'd lost have a habit of coming back to us. Sometimes when we aren't looking for them. I pick up sea glass because it makes me believe in things like hope and clarity. On one afternoon, I find two rare pieces, one orange and one bright blue. As I look at them side by side in my palm, I am transported to a time when I saw those colours in a different landscape. Another island, equal in mystery but far from the one which raised me. Maui. Breathtaking and serene. I spent time there years ago and now it comes back to me on the surging tide. How, at the summit of the volcano of Haleakalā

I stood on the rim of the circular crater valley before sunrise and watched as the fire of dawn ignited the carpet of mist at my feet, turning it to dazzling gold. As the sun ascended, the mists burned away to reveal on the one hand tropical rainforest descending down the outside of the volcano and on the other, a wide desert valley, the wall dropping away steeply and a small, stony trail inviting explorers down. The warm desert sand and brilliant blue sky were mirrored by the sea glass which now lay in my hand. Vibrant orange and blue.

Hawaii was a land of such intensity, experiencing it was like living in a state of multi-layered synaesthesia, where senses merged into each other so that sound, colour and form became one. I first encountered Huna here, the Hawaiian shamanic teachings which are founded in the deepest respect for the interwoven nature of land, people and spirit. These are inseparable elements. Yet somehow, we have separated ourselves from spirit and from the land. We have severed our connection and in doing so subjected ourselves to disharmony and disease. We cannot make real progress until we reconnect.

For a time, I too walked the grey path. It was where I needed to go. But I was in danger of identifying myself too much with the path I was on. I walked with all the colours of Hawaii, my mother's garden and the ocean currents carried on the inside as precious cargo in a ship's hold. But our treasures are best lived, not stored away. Our most valuable learnings can show us how to find our direction, but you can't navigate if you've packed up the sextant and stowed it away. Only when I returned to Cornwall and felt my connection to the land renew itself did the memories of Hawaii and the teachings of Huna come back to me. Land, people and spirit. Interwoven. Entwined. Every element connected. When we are one with the land, then we have found the state of being home.

Sometimes the tide brings us random beauty, other times it brings us secret stories, or magic hidden in plain sight. Like driftwood. I've always liked driftwood. It seems to tell stories. It came from trees but it has been in the ocean, travelling among fishes, whales and birds, under the sun and the stars. It is not of the place where its physical life appeared to begin. It has become more elemental than that. Pieces of driftwood remind me of interesting people, each with a story to tell. Each beautiful in their own way. Different yet washed by the same tides. I find wonderful small pieces high up on the sand at the uppermost reach of the waves after winter storms. I start to see ideas forming from the strange shapes and colours. It feels like the world is becoming one of my paintings around me. Dreaming… We are dreaming…

Red Kite told me to make beautiful things, my hedge dream told me to find my way to the home I wanted using my hands, the sea told me to weave the life I sought and my mother had told me always to be myself and love the wild. Not to compromise.

I learn to wire-weave; I buy silver and copper wire, without allowing myself to worry about whether I can afford new equipment to try and let my fingers follow the patterns of the waves, turning it in flowing lines around sea-glass finds, making pendants inspired by the beach. I start to wood-carve, because I always wanted to as a child and now it seems right not to wait. I let the driftwood speak to me and use it unaltered, taking pleasure in handling it in ways which honour the natural shapes within. I start teaching myself to engrave different surfaces with heat, using a pyrography pen. It feels elemental and healthy to learn new creative techniques. I let the land, sea and sky flow directly from my subconscious, through my hands. I offer myself to the wild and the ancestors for their voices to speak through mine.

Chapter 35
One

Silvery-white sea campions carpet the feet of the Watcher rock where my mother's ashes have mingled with the earth and my hopes had mingled with the sky. Fragile flowers and enduring stone. A skylark soars, singing, pouring its unfettered heart into the space between us. Then another. A cascade of notes spilling across the cliffs, shockingly pure. A tiny, coppery-brown beetle, on wispy legs, wanders delicately around a tuft of candy-pink thrift.

A silver-grey seagull floats by, suspended on the updraught rising from the cliff edge. No headstone inscribed with words of remembrance marks the place. No sweet memorial to tell the world I loved you. But there where the spirit of life runs, strong as the flood of light, there I dare to hope that I gave you something better.

What more enduring headstone could I find than something born 400 million years ago? When no words suffice, what better voice could there be than the music of skylarks and the sounding sea? When all other headstones have fallen and their words have worn away to nothing, yours will show that I kept my word and brought you home. The griffin-being stands watch. He who has faced the sea in such proud regard since the sea has been here, he is your headstone. No cut marble polished and cold for you, but the living rock, pulsing with the heartbeat of the earth. Your ashes became part of the griffin's home. I am proud that we were here together.

Time slows down here, or maybe it is the idea of it which melts away. The illusions weaken. Lose their hold. The set cast of seconds, minutes and hours which frames our lives in such rigid lines and drives our dreams into corners, to gather dust, starts to unravel. Life comes in moments and each one holds forever. Time stops being flat or straight. It becomes deep, like the Universe full of stars. Moments expand to eternities.

Monty looks out across the sea, with the same expression as the griffin-being. For a moment it seems strange, before I stop and realise that it isn't really strange at all. We are one. The same life-force that flows through all we see is in us also. The melody behind the notes, the ocean underneath the waves. We are one.

It is three years now, since I first stood in my driveway with Monty on that frosty night in the Fens, holding him close and sensing that maybe together we could find a better way of living. Three years since I first started remembering how to listen to the whispering wild. But somehow that moment and this are directly fused. Any other choice in that driveway, any other turn in the road and we might not be here. All the new directions and possibilities that sprang into life are not just me and Monty and the subject of our book, they are part of you. Because you too are listening now. Because you read this far.

The voice of the Universe is strange. Indescribably vast. Yet it speaks through the narrowest of moments. It can stop time altogether. Or make us realise it was never real. Sunlight gleams on a furry bee's iridescent wings. The same sunlight twinkles on fluffy bubbles of sea spray, flying through the air. That sunlight reaches my eyes and Monty's in the 8 minutes 20 seconds it took for it to arrive here from the sun 149.6 million kilometres away. Somewhere out there, in the distant reaches of the Universe, a star goes supernova, its core collapsing in a quarter of a second. Forming and then scattering the same elements from which our physical bodies are made. In the time it takes our hearts to beat, an eternity can be born.

We have stardust bodies and infinite spirits. Our eyes and the rest of our bodies, the rocks we sit on and the bee with the gossamer-thin wings, we are all made of elements which formed in the hearts of stars hundreds of thousands of years ago. Each atom of our bodies holds the blueprint of the Universe. We are one.

Into the Whispering Wild

We do not just hear the voice of the wild, we are made from it, we were born to hear it. What is wilder than a star? It doesn't matter where we were born on this planet. All of us came from the heart of the stars. It doesn't matter who we called our parents, whether we loved them and they us, or not. Together we are travellers; when we look up into the night sky and starlight falls upon our eyes, it is our ancient birthplace which illuminates us.

Everything that makes up our physical bodies came from the stars. And the non-physical? That is mystery. We all navigate our journey for ourselves. I can only tell you what the wild said. I can share what Monty told me. My wise young friend who walks beside me. Underpinning all else they said, there was one clear, recurring message. "Look closer!" they told me. "The answers are within."

I walk the paths outside Lizard village with Monty at all hours, looking closer, observing the tiny fluctuations in light and the details of the landscape. Twisted gorse bushes, old half-hidden stone walls telling stories of other lives. The timeless roar of eternity is everywhere. Palpable. All we have to do to hear it is just stop *not* hearing it. It is not the sea song; it is what pulses behind it. It is not the bird-song; it reverberates in the silence through which their song is flowing. Maybe it can be heard everywhere, but for me, there is nowhere I hear it clearer than here.

It tells me stories now. It teaches. I am becoming a storyteller of wild places. Mists and sunshine. Blackbirds and tawny owls. Creamy yarrow and purple vetch, golden coltsfoot. All finding their way onto paper. Happily, randomly, Monty and I join with the heart of the land. We breathe it in. Entwined by our breath with the real world and each other.

The wild world has funny ways of challenging us, sometimes. Stupidly, I let Monty get fleas. I have always given him flea and tick chews, which normally work fine through most months with just some extra products during the summer. But stress causes forgetfulness and before I know it, there they are, in his fur. Not many, just one or two. But one or two can turn into a few hundred very quickly and they can't be left unchecked. No matter how many times I get rid of them, there are always just one or two more. Wild or not, I don't welcome fleas! I'm all for being at one with nature but I am not about to let parasites drink Monty's blood, or mine!

I research natural flea treatments; I learn and I hoover. I hoover with a vengeance. "Oh, this is ridiculous! I'm not going to be grateful for fleas!" I tell the Universe, as I hoover for the umpteenth time. But I am laughing as I say it. "Really?" it challenges. I swear I hear it laughing back.

"Well, Monty certainly isn't!"

"So, deal with them then!"

I hoover. I brush. Then I hoover some more. As I do, I feel better. It becomes easier to think and focus. I do things I have been putting off. I notice it is feeling easier to breathe. I start clearing out extra items so that I can hoover more effectively. I remember cleansing and clearing rituals. I practise the visualisations of letting go. Banishing what isn't working. Dust symbolises old emotions. Each flea represents a doubt. Feeding on our life-force. Creeping in unnoticed and sucking away the energy of my guardian muse.

As I brush Monty, we bond, ever more. I brush small amounts of coconut oil through his fur, working it through the soft feathers under his belly and down the backs of his legs. His silky fur, which was already something of an obsession for me, shines like polished ebony. Grass seeds and burrs, the bane of cocker spaniel owners everywhere, fall from his coat easily at the slightest touch of a comb because there were no tangles anywhere. Monty, who has always loved being brushed, is in bliss with all the attention and comfort.

The more I get cross with the arrival of the fleas, the more determinedly they seemed to hang on. Once I relax into being happy caring for Monty, all of a sudden, they are gone, without a trace. I haven't quite managed to be grateful for the fleas, but I am grateful for what they taught me. Monty is just grateful that I got rid of them.

Chapter 36
Two

A tiny golden hoverfly rises from the grass under the apple trees. Iridescent wings beating almost faster than the power of sight. "Good morning, Hoverfly!" I greet it cheerfully. The hoverfly doesn't answer, it just hovers enigmatically in front of me. For a moment, I am entranced by its wings. So rapid! Two hundred beats per second. I can't comprehend moving that fast. But as I try, I drop into those fragments of a second and time stands still again, the same way it does when I hear the tide. I keep falling through gaps between time. Between the waves. Between the beats of a hoverfly's wings. Perhaps it did answer, after all.

New and old stop having the same meanings. I'm not sure if they have any meaning. Is this what dying feels like? If so it's OK. The falling away of worn-out structures and explanations for the world which never quite fit anyway. It feels like expanding and diminishing at the same time. Some bits of me are fading away to nothing, others are growing and stretching out into the trees and the sea. Always, the sea. The wild waves surge and change the beach underfoot with every moment. I feel the shifts and adjust my balance, wondering what else in my life I needed to rebalance? Is worrying about the things I don't have sending me off-balance? Like in the dojo, over-reaching to an opponent outside my circle. I can almost hear my instructors, "Centre yourself! Balance is in the centre." It has taken this journey to show me what they meant.

I head for the path to the High Place. The centre! Where we balance from. Combat, life, walking, all one. I used to train barefoot.

No wonder I lost my sense of balance when I stopped. Every day becomes a journey of returning to the centre of life. I stop focusing on achievements and start focusing upon balance. "Where am I off-balance?" I ask Life, the Universe, the Ancestors or whatever that wordless voice is that speaks from behind the waves and wind. A small bee searches energetically for nectar among the fluffy pink thrift, while the tiniest brown beetle climbs a blade of grass, poised, shining on the summit as if contemplating where to go next. The only way left is up. It teeters, waves its legs and I wonder if it is looking back down where it came from. Then it takes flight. A seagull drifts effortlessly by, uplifted by invisible currents of air. Subtly adjusting its wings to the strength of the breeze, it turns to face the open water and rises higher. Another joins it. They balance on the shifting wind as if playing for a moment and then together they head towards the south.

I watch their silvery-grey forms as they become smaller, disappearing from view until they vanish into the brilliance. Something about it speaks to me, in a form without words. Some inner knowing about flight. About rising higher. We can see further horizons if we lift ourselves up.

The seagull found someone to fly with. I like to fly solo. I'm comfortable in my own space. But life is short. If I'm being unreasonable then maybe I should do it wholeheartedly and let myself want everything. Why not? Life is ours for learning and experiencing, but we learn more when we share ideas. It is all the conversations and the unexpected insights of being with others, random, like sea glass, which let us test our own creative strength, as birds on the breeze. Sometimes when we lift each other higher, we see further horizons to aim for than we might otherwise have sought. Is it possible, maybe I don't have to fly alone?

The inner critic tells me it is the wrong time to get into a relationship. I tell it to be quiet and ask it, "What's the right time anyway? The world is full of people waiting for the right time to do things. In the end the right time never comes. We've got to stop waiting for the right time and make right the time we have." My inner critic lapses into silence.

For once, it seems content with the reply.

Early in the morning I wander with Monty, through the long grass, every stem glistening with drenching dew. Monty leaps and snuffles, enjoying the refreshing coolness, sending silvery sparkles in all directions from his paws. Ears flapping happily up and down. It's impossible to be critical or negative while watching a spaniel playing. They embody the joy of living, wrapped up in little furry bodies with floppy ears, waggy tails and silly grins.

"What do you want from a relationship?" Judy asks me as we watch our dogs playing together, while we talk about assorted things. "I want to be with someone who is going to be kind to my dog!" I replied. "Someone who understands why he sleeps on the bed and doesn't say 'Ugh I couldn't put up with that!' But rather, 'Obviously. Where else would he sleep? That's where dogs belong, next to us.'"

She gives me space to think so I pause then continue. "I want to be with someone who isn't going to think I've fucked up, or dropped out, because I'm living in a caravan. Someone who sees that what I am at the moment isn't what I've always been or what I'm going to be. We have to be able to grow together, otherwise what's the point? Relationships are about helping each other learn and grow, not trying to keep our partners what they were once or what we think we want them to be. I want to be with someone who won't look at my life and say, 'You left everything behind,' but who says 'Where are you going? I want to come along for the adventure!'"

We mooch through the meadow, long grass stems tickling our legs and Monty jumping around, excitedly hunting mice, most of which I'm sure are in his imagination. "I'm hoping that person will look at my work and understand what I'm trying to do," I explain. "The kind of relationship where my partner can get behind what I'm about and I can back them up just as much too. I don't mean to sound like I think it's all about work, because I really don't. But what we create, well, it's important. It's about who we choose to be in this world and how we grow." I stop myself, before I start prattling on about seagulls.

Judy regards me slowly. Listening. For a moment I wonder if

I've said something strange. It wouldn't be the first time. "Well, that must be possible," she suggested. *Possible*, there was that word again, echoing the voice of the sea. She has set me wondering what else might be possible. Why do we forget 'possible' so easily? A seagull doesn't question the possibility of flight or whether the wind will blow, it just senses the horizon, the waves and sky… and flies.

"Maybe we can be more like seagulls?" I ask.

She smiles. Monty wags his tail.

Chapter 37
Now

Where are we now? *Now*, that is the word where magic lives. Now is our circle of power. Now is where all things coincide. Now is choice and I choose to be here. Yes, I am still on the Lizard with Monty. Do I know if I will be here next year, or for the rest of my life? Do I know if I will be flying alone? No, I don't. But I know how to be here now and for now, that will have to be enough. Do I know if I can navigate my way safely to a place called Home? No, but I do know I have come through storms already because I couldn't let down my faithful dog. That is a choice too. Not letting someone down. I've chosen not to let myself down. I will see where that choice takes me.

Maybe you will find us in the Lys Ardh. If it calls you. In the wild afternoons on rocky shorelines and high, green moors or in breeze-kissed early mornings on a coastal path somewhere high above the sea. Perhaps Monty will come running up to you on a beach somewhere, all covered in sand and ears flapping as he jumps around for the joy of living. Maybe you will come here or perhaps your journey will lead you a different way, to a different shore. Perhaps mine will. All roads entwine. Maybe we will meet in dreams, somewhere in the Now.

When I came here, I was searching for more than just a home or the tangible places. I still need a physical home for me and Monty but the journey here has become about something more. I can't leave Cornwall. If I can't leave then I will have to stay and if I have to stay then it will have to work out. Somehow. I trust the magic that brought me here with my dog. My wild-sense tingles in response to the idea. "That's right," agrees the inner nomad. "That's right!"

"That's right!" confirms my mother's spirit. "You don't know what you can do until you try." I sense her encouragement. "Even if you think you don't have enough, you started out in this life with a lot less and you have come so far! You took all the things I taught you and you made something of them. You wove them into a life that I could never have foreseen. Look at everything you've done so far. You chose that! You wove that life from the colours of all that you knew."

"You gave me all my best colours. I miss you."

"OK, then let's weave something together! I'm still here. I'm part of you. I surround you like the wild. Let's weave something beautiful!"

We set out to greet the light, as the sun rises. I turn to the wild path, facing the dawn. Breath in my lungs and dog at my side. Skylarks begin to ascend. We step into the wild space at the meeting point of worlds. From somewhere overhead I hear the voice of Sky Dragon calling, "Use the gift!" From somewhere close by, I hear the voice of my mother, murmuring "Be yourself, always."

The motion and stillness of the Universe align. Perhaps we are always at the start of a new journey if we choose to be. All we have to do is notice the doorway of choice it begins with. The doorway of now. Now... Manawa. Now is the moment of power.

Into the whispering wild we head. Senses outstretched into the pattern of the world. Every day, every breath turns the kaleidoscope world a fraction, sending new possibilities spinning.

"Are you ready?" asks the wild.

"Are you ready?" asks the inner nomad.

Monty nudges my hand and wags his tail.

I stand on the path and I reply, "Let's see!"